HARBRACE COLLEGE WORKBOOK

FORM 7A

$395

HARBRACE COLLEGE WORKBOOK

WORKBOOK

FORM 7A

Sheila Y. Graham

Galveston College

**in consultation with
Mrs. John C. Hodges**

Harcourt Brace Jovanovich, Inc.

New York / Chicago / San Francisco / Atlanta

Contents

MECHANICS

PUNCTUATION

SPELLING AND DICTION

EFFECTIVE SENTENCES

Preface

To the Instructor

This book is frankly utilitarian. It begins with sentence analysis and stresses the basic principles of the clear English sentence. It keeps grammatical terms to a minimum, introducing only those principles most useful in writing.

Arrangement   The materials are arranged under numbers **1** to **30**—omitting **8**, which is covered in the preface to the student—to parallel the first thirty sections of the *Harbrace College Handbook,* Seventh Edition. But these materials may be used to supplement any handbook, or they may be used independently. The explanatory pages preceding each section enable the book to stand on its own. The order in which the materials should be studied, as well as the speed with which they should be covered, will naturally be determined by the instructor in the light of the first written work or of diagnostic tests. The needs of the class will determine whether an assignment will consist of the normal single exercise, of only a part of one, or—at the other extreme—of several exercises. Some of the exercises can be done orally in class.

Exercises   The subject matter of the exercises has been drawn from a field that concerns everyone—ecology. The exercises give the student an opportunity to explore what is happening in ecology while he is working to improve his composition.

The Dictionary   One reason for varying the order of the exercises may be the need at the opening of the course for a review of the uses of the dictionary. Unless each member of the class owns a good dictionary and knows how to use it effectively for spelling, pronunciation, meanings of words, and other information, the first assignment may very well be Exercise 19-1, Using the Dictionary.

Spelling   Ignorance of the correct spelling of ordinary words is now, and will probably continue to be, the one universally accepted sign of the uneducated man. After the student has reached senior high school or college, he cannot count on much class time being devoted to spelling. Correct spelling is then his own responsibility. He can make steady improvement in his spelling by listing and mastering every word he has misspelled. The list should be carefully kept in the blanks at the end of this book. If the list grows to considerable length before the class comes to Section **18**, the student can further improve his spelling by analyzing his own misspellings in connection with Exercises 18-1 through 18-5. Any poor speller who carefully follows the spelling program provided in this book will be pleased with the marked improvement in his spelling.

Writing The written work of the course will enable the student to carry over into the sentences of paragraphs and longer papers the principles of good writing mastered through the sentences of the workbook. To correct his written work the student may be referred to the explanatory sections, each of which has a number and a symbol derived from the *Harbrace College Handbook,* Seventh Edition.

To the Student

Preparation of Your Manuscript

Materials Unless you are given other instructions, use standard theme paper, 8½ by 11 inches, with lines about half an inch apart. Use black or blue-black ink. For typewritten themes use regular typewriter paper, 8½ by 11 inches. Submit typewritten themes only if you do your own typing.

Arrangement on the Page Leave sufficient margins—about an inch and a half at left and top, an inch at right and bottom—to prevent a crowded appearance. The ruled lines on theme paper indicate the proper margins at left and top. In typewritten themes use double spacing. Indent the first lines of paragraphs uniformly, about an inch in longhand and five spaces in typewritten copy. Leave no long gap at the end of any line except the last one in the paragraph. Use Arabic numerals in the upper right-hand corner to mark all pages after the first. Center the title on the page about an inch and a half from the top or on the first ruled line. Leave the next line blank and begin the first paragraph on the third line. In this way the title will be made to stand out from the text. Endorse the theme in the way designated by your instructor.

Legibility Make each word a distinct unit: join all the letters of a word and leave adequate space before beginning the next word. Shape each letter distinctly. Avoid flourishes. Many pages of manuscript generally artistic and attractive to the eye are almost illegible. Dot each *i*, not some other letter nearby. Cross each *t*, not an adjoining *h* or some other letter. Make dots and periods real dots, not small circles. Let all capitals stand out distinctly as capitals and keep all small letters down to the average height of other small letters. Remember that you will not be present to tell the reader which letters you intend to be capitals, which to be small letters.

Syllabication Never divide a word of a single syllable at the end of a line. Divide other words only between syllables (parts pronounced as separate units of a word). Do not confuse the reader by setting off an *-ed* pronounced as a part of the preceding syllable (as in *forced, opened, reared*). The simplest way to check syllabication is to refer to the word in the dictionary. For detailed rules regarding syllabication, consult an unabridged dictionary.

You learn how to write chiefly by correcting your own errors. Corrections made for you are of comparatively little value. Therefore the instructor points out the errors but allows you to make the actual revision for yourself. The instructor usually indicates a necessary correction by a number (or a symbol) marked in the margin of the theme opposite the error. If a word is misspelled, the number **18** (or the symbol **sp**) will be used; if there is a sentence fragment, the number **2** (or the symbol **frag**); if there is a faulty reference of a pronoun, the number **28** (or the symbol **ref**). Consult the text (see the guides on the inside covers), master the principle underlying each correction, and make the necessary revisions in red. Draw one red line through words to be deleted, but allow such words to remain legible in order that the instructor may compare the revised form with the original.

The Comma   After the number **12** in the margin you should take special care to supply the appropriate letter (**a**, **b**, **c**, or **d**) from the explanatory section on pages 71–78 to show why the comma is needed. The act of inserting a comma teaches little; understanding why it is required in a particular situation is a definite step toward mastery of the comma. (Your instructor may require that you pinpoint each of your own errors by supplying the appropriate letter after every number he writes in the margin.)

Specimen Paragraph from a Student Theme

Marked by the Instructor with Symbols

cs   Making photographs for newspapers is hard work, it is not

2/   the romantic carefree adventure glorified in motion pictures

    and fiction books. For every great moment recorded by the

sp   stareing eye of the camera, there are twenty routine assign-

ref   ments that must be handled in the same efficient manner. He

    must often overcome great hardships. The work continues for

sub   long hours. It must meet the deadline. At times he is called

    upon to risk his own life to secure a picture. To the news-

frag   paper photographer, getting his picture being the most impor-

    tant thing.

Marked by the Instructor with Numbers

3   Making photographs for newspapers is hard work, it is not

/2   the romantic carefree adventure glorified in motion pictures

      and fiction books. For every great moment recorded by the

18   stareing eye of the camera, there are twenty routine assign-

28   ments that must be handled in the same efficient manner. He

      must often overcome great hardships. The work continues for

24

      long hours. It must meet the deadline. At times he is called

      upon to risk his own life to secure a picture. To the news-

2   paper photographer, getting his picture being the most impor-

      tant thing.

Corrected by the Student

3   Making photographs for newspapers is hard work/; it is not

/2C   the romantic, carefree adventure glorified in motion pictures

      and fiction books. For every great moment recorded by the

      staring

18   ~~stareing~~ eye of the camera, there are twenty routine assign-

                                                   The

28   ments that must be handled in the same efficient manner. ~~He~~

      newspaper photographer must often overcome great

      ~~must often overcome great hardships. The work continues~~ for

24   *hardships and work long hours to meet the deadline.*

      ~~long hours. It must meet the deadline.~~ At times he is called

      upon to risk his own life to secure a picture. To the news-

                                         is

2   paper photographer, getting his picture ~~being~~ the most impor-

      tant thing.

Sentence Sense   ss 1

1

The first step in learning to write clearly and effectively is to understand the sentence.

1a   Learn to recognize the verb, the nucleus of the sentence.

Without a verb no group of words is grammatically a sentence.

> a college student
> a college student with no shoes on
> A college student with no shoes on *rode* the motorcycle.

Only the third of these groups of words really makes a complete statement. The word *rode* is the vital word. Omit it, and the sentence becomes merely a fragment—not a sentence at all.

A verb may be recognized by its form and its meaning.

Form   When converted from present to past tense, nearly all verbs change form: *ride—rode, am—was, love—loved*. When converted from first person to third person singular, in the present tense, all verbs change form: *I ride—he rides, I am—he is, I love—he loves*. All verbs in the progressive tense end in *-ing: I am riding, I am being, I am loving*. Such form changes are called inflections (or conjugations).

Meaning   A verb may express action (He *rides* wildly), indicate a state of being (He *is* sick), assert something (He *loves* peace), make a statement (He *is* riding), ask a question (*Is* he *riding?*), or give a command (*Ride* now).

Verb phrases   A verb phrase (or cluster) is made up of a verb and one or more auxiliaries, or "helping verbs": *rides > is riding, has been riding, should have been riding*. Common auxiliaries are *am, is, are, was, were, be, been, has, have, had, do, does, did, may, might, must, shall, will, would, should, ought to, can,* and *could*.

The words that make up a verb phrase are often separated (He *did* not really *ride* the camel. *Could* he *have ridden* the camel?). Neither the adverb *not* nor its contraction (did*n't*) is ever a part of the verb.

Verbs and particles   Sometimes a particle like *with, up,* or *up with* accompanies the verb to make a single unit of meaning.

> Astronauts must *put up with* many inconveniences.
> They *put in* many months of grueling study and practice.

1

1b Learn to recognize subjects and objects of verbs.

Subjects In every grammatically complete sentence the verb has a subject. However, in a command or a request the subject is often implied rather than actually included in the sentence: Ride quickly (*You* ride quickly).

In a sentence that asks a question, the subject can be found more easily if the sentence is rephrased in the form of a statement:

Did the *astronauts* reach the moon?
The *astronauts* did reach the moon.

The complete subject is the subject and all words associated with it; likewise, the complete predicate is the verb along with associated words and phrases.

> *Complete Subject*   *Complete Predicate*
> El Greco, the Greek painter,   lived in Spain.

Objects Often the verb has an object—a word or group of words that receives, or is in some way affected by, the action of the verb.

Thomas Jefferson wrote the *Declaration of Independence*.
He also founded the *University of Virginia*.

Occasionally verbs such as *buy, bring, give, lend, offer, sell,* or *send* have not only a direct object but also an indirect object which states to whom or for whom something is done:

You can't teach an old *dog* new tricks.
He gave the *poor* food.

A few verbs, such as *is*, do not take objects, but complements which refer to the subject:

Leonardo was a *painter*. [*Painter* is not the object of *was*, but refers to the subject *Leonardo*.]
He also became an *inventor*. [*Inventor* refers to *He*.]

Tests for Subject and Object

In a sentence subjects and objects may be recognized by form, meaning, and position.

Form Subjects and objects of verbs are either nouns or noun substitutes such as pronouns. The most commonly used pronouns have one form for the subject and a different form for the object: *I—me, he—him, she—her, they—them, who—whom*. Nearly all nouns (words used to name persons, places, things, ideas, or actions) change form to indicate number: *boy—boys, man—men, city—cities*. The articles *a, an,* and *the* are sometimes called "noun determiners" or "noun indicators," because they regularly point to a following noun: a *boy*, an *apple*, the big *apple*.

Meaning To find the subject, simply ask in connection with the verb, "Who or what?"

The father bought his children expensive presents.

"Who bought? The *father* bought." *Father* is thus shown to be the subject.

To find the object, ask "Whom or what?" received the action or effect of the verb. "The father bought what? The father bought *presents*." So *presents* is proved to be the object. Another characteristic of the object is that it can be made the subject of the passive form of the verb. "*Presents* were bought by the father."

The indirect object is shown by asking "To whom or for whom?" (or "To what or for what?") something is done: "For whom did the father buy presents? The father bought presents for his *children*." Thus *children* is shown to be the indirect object.

Position   A third way to recognize subjects and objects is to become thoroughly familiar with the usual word order of English sentences. This is usually subject—verb—object. Observe the importance of word order in determining meaning.

PATTERN 1   SUBJECT—VERB.

The campus *newspaper is published* daily.
Opinions about campus violence *vary*.

PATTERN 2   SUBJECT—VERB—OBJECT.

Newspapers have different editorial *outlooks*.
One should read several *newspapers*.

PATTERN 3   SUBJECT—VERB—INDIRECT OBJECT—DIRECT OBJECT.

The *judges presented* the winning relay *team* its *trophy*.
The *team showed us* a fine *example* of baton-handling.

For patterns with subject complements, see **4b.**

The preceding three sentence patterns may be varied in several ways, primarily by the use of *there* (an expletive or introductory word) and by a shift to interrogative (question) word order. Notice that the order of the sentence parts changes with such variation.

There was a new bowl added this year.   [Variation of Pattern 1]
What do you think about astrology?   [Variation of Pattern 2]
Did the director give his actors believable stage movements?   [Variation of Pattern 3]

Compounds   Subjects, verbs, and objects may be compound.

Michelangelo and *Leonardo* were famous artists.
Michelangelo *painted* and *sculpted*.
Leonardo produced both *art* and various *inventions*.

1c   Learn to recognize all the parts of speech.

Words are usually grouped into eight word classes, or "parts of speech," according to their uses in the sentence.

Parts of Speech	Uses in the Sentence	Examples
1. Verbs	Indicators of action or state of being (often link subjects and complements)	Tom *hit* the curve. Mary *was* tired. He *is* a senator.
2. Nouns	Subjects, objects, complements	*Kay* gave *Ron* the *book* of *poems.*
3. Pronouns	Substitutes for nouns	*He* will return *it* to *her* later.
4. Adjectives	Modifiers of nouns and noun substitutes	*The long* poem is *the best.*
5. Adverbs	Modifiers of verbs, adjectives, adverbs, or whole clauses	sang *loudly* a *very* sad song *entirely too* fast
6. Prepositions	Words used before nouns and noun substitutes to relate them to other words in the sentence	*to* the lake *in* a hurry *with* no thought
7. Conjunctions	Connectives	win *or* lose good *but* dull Come *as* you are.
8. Interjections	Expressions of emotion (unrelated grammatically to the rest of the sentence)	*Woe* is me! *Ouch! Imagine!*

The dictionary lists the word class or classes in which a given word may be used, but the actual classification of a word depends on its use in a sentence.

1d Learn to recognize phrases and subordinate clauses.

PHRASES

A phrase is a group of related words, without both a subject and a predicate, that is used as a noun, a verb, or a modifier (adjective or adverb).

NOUN PHRASE *To read* is *to discover truth.* [The noun phrases act as subject and complement.]

VERB PHRASE He *has read* all the novels of Dostoevski.

MODIFYING PHRASE The English novel *as a genre* made its appearance *during the eighteenth century.* [The first modifying phrase is an adjective; the second, an adverb.]

Phrases may also be classified as prepositional phrases or verbal phrases.

Prepositional phrases The prepositional phrase is a related word group that begins with a preposition and concludes with a noun called the object of the preposition. Prepositional phrases normally function as modifiers, and they often occur in groups.

> The girl *with no date for the dance* sat *in her dormitory room.*   [*With no date* modifies *girl; for the dance* modifies *date;* and *in her dormitory room* modifies *sat.*]

Verbal phrases A phrase introduced by a participle, a gerund, or an infinitive is called a verbal phrase. Participles, gerunds, and infinitives are derived from verbs and are much like verbs in that they have different tenses, can have subjects and objects, and can be modified by adverbs. But they are not true verbs; they cannot function as the only verb form in the sentence.

> VERB   The girl *made* an Indian headband.
>
> VERBAL   The girl *making* an Indian headband has lived on a reservation. [The verbal *making* requires another verb form in the sentence— *has lived.*]

Verbal phrases—participial, gerund, and infinitive—function as nouns or modifiers in sentences.

> PARTICIPIAL PHRASE The students *wearing the orange and white caps* are freshmen.   [The participial phrase functions as an adjective modifying students.]
>
> GERUND PHRASE *Learning a second language* requires perseverance.   [The gerund phrase functions as a noun, the subject of the sentence.]
>
> INFINITIVE PHRASE The one thing *never to forget* is *to hold your head high.* [The first infinitive phrase functions as an adjective modifying *thing;* the second functions as a noun, the complement of the verb *is.*]

Notice that both the present participle and the gerund end in -*ing* and that they can be distinguished only by their use in the sentence: the participle is an adjective and the gerund is a noun.

Infinitive phrases are made up of *to* plus the verb form and may function as either nouns or modifiers.

CLAUSES

A clause is a group of related words containing a verb and its subject. If a clause can stand alone as a simple sentence, it is called a main (or independent) clause; if it cannot, it is called a subordinate (or dependent) clause.

> The students waited *while the speaker searched for the chalk.*   [Main clause followed by a subordinate clause]

If these clauses are separated, we have a simple sentence and a sentence fragment.

The students waited.   [Simple sentence]
While the speaker searched for the chalk.   [Sentence fragment]

The subordinating conjunction *while* makes the clause that follows it subordinate. (Some other words that frequently introduce subordinate clauses are *when, if, since, because, although, whoever, who, which,* and *that.*)

Subordinate clauses may function in sentences either as modifiers (adjectives or adverbs) or as nouns.

Adverb clauses   Adverb clauses frequently modify verbs, but they may also modify adjectives, adverbs, verbals, prepositional phrases, or even main clauses. An adverb clause, like an individual adverb, may be placed at various positions in the sentence.

> *When the dog was found,* everyone sighed with relief.   [A comma usually follows an introductory adverb clause.]
> Everyone sighed with relief *when the dog was found.*   [Usually no comma is used with a concluding adverb clause.]

Adjective clauses   Adjective clauses, which are normally introduced by a relative pronoun like *who, which,* or *that,* are usually located immediately after the nouns or pronouns they modify.

> The dog, *which we finally found,* was unharmed.

Sometimes the relative pronoun is omitted if the adjective clause is short.

> **The speaker** *(whom)* **we wanted** was not available.   [The relative pronoun is understood but not stated in the sentence.]

Noun clauses   Noun clauses have the same functions that nouns have.

> *Whoever would speak on short notice* was invited.   [The noun clause is used as the subject of the verb.]

1e   Learn to recognize various types of sentence.

Sentences may be classified structurally as simple, compound, complex, or compound-complex. A simple sentence is made up of one main clause.

> The Borghese Gardens are free to the public.

A compound sentence is made up of two or more main clauses.

> The Borghese Gardens are free to the public, and many Romans visit them.

A complex sentence is made up of one main clause and at least one subordinate clause.

> The Borghese Gardens, which are two miles square, are free to the public.

A compound-complex sentence is made up of two or more main clauses and at least one subordinate clause.

> The Borghese Gardens, which are two miles square, are free to the public, and many Romans visit them.

Subject and verb in simple sentences

NAME _____ SCORE _____

DIRECTIONS   In the following sentences underline the subject once, the verb twice. Then enter each subject and verb in the blanks at the right, noting that subject and verb always agree in number. In the third blank write the number of the sentence pattern followed from the three patterns given in **1b**.

EXAMPLE   *Subject*   *Verb*   *Pattern*

In the last ten years the science of ecology has emerged.

_____science_____   _has emerged_   ___1___

1. Many species of animal life are disappearing.

_____   _____   _____

2. According to ecologists man is included on the list of endangered species.

_____   _____   _____

3. For too long man has thoughtlessly exploited his environment.

_____   _____   _____

4. Now the environment is giving man his punishment.

_____   _____   _____

5. Does any clean air remain?

_____   _____   _____

6. Which waterways has man not polluted?

_____   _____   _____

7. Are most of our natural resources not almost depleted?

_____   _____   _____

8. How many species of animal life has man destroyed?

_____   _____   _____

9. Has man not ravaged his planet in too many ways?

_____   _____   _____

10. Should nature not eventually strike back?

_____   _____   _____

11. Will nature give man much more time?

_____   _____   _____

12. There are new environmental problems encountered each year.

_____   _____   _____

13. Man must first recognize the problems.

_____   _____   _____

14. Then perhaps he can find solutions.

_____   _____   _____

15. But no solution comes easily.

_____   _____   _____

16. Many sacrifices will be called for.

_____   _____   _____

17. Patterns of living must be altered.

_____   _____   _____

18. Ecologists do not promise people a comfortable future.

_____   _____   _____

19. But, hopefully, man will not disappear.

_____   _____   _____

20. The future we must plan for now.

_____   _____   _____

21. The time of living only for present convenience has passed.

_____   _____   _____

22. This book presents various views about environmental problems and their solutions.

_____   _____   _____

23. It shows us the ecologists' opinions.

_____   _____   _____

24. Do we not owe the ecologists a hearing?

_____   _____   _____

25. Attention to their findings may save our planet from destruction.

_____   _____   _____

Subject and verb in simple sentences

NAME _____ SCORE _____

DIRECTIONS   In the following sentences underline the subject once, the verb twice. Then enter each subject and verb in the blanks at the right. Some of the subjects and verbs are compound. (Note that subject and verb always agree in number.)

	Subject	Verb
EXAMPLE		
Our air, water, and land have been polluted.	*air* *water* *land*	*have been polluted*

1. One of the ecologists' main concerns is air pollution. _____ _____

2. Pesticides, radioactive fallout, and automobile and industrial fumes have all played major roles in polluting our air. _____ _____

3. How contaminated is our air? _____ _____

4. The amount of pollution varies throughout our country. _____ _____

5. Major cities like New York and Los Angeles naturally suffer the most from air pollution. _____ _____

6. Large areas of smog around our industrial cities are seen by airline pilots from seventy miles away. _____ _____

7. But even small cities and towns experience air pollution. _____ _____

8. There is no clean air left anywhere. _____ _____

9. Do you know the major contributor to air pollution? _____ _____

10. Exhausts from automobiles are our most serious polluters. _____ _____

11. According to a 1969 Senate report, at least 60 percent of all air pollution may be blamed on the automobile. _____ _____

12. Everyone knows and fears the effects of carbon monoxide in a closed area. _____ _____

13. In the open, carbon monoxide from gasoline engines operates more subtly. _____ _____

14. This deadly pollutant reduces the capacity of the blood to carry oxygen. _____ _____

15. Thus both the heart and the respiratory system are adversely affected by carbon monoxide. _____ _____

16. There are other poisons in automobile exhaust fumes. _____ _____

17. One of these is lead. _____ _____

18. The lead from automobile exhausts can build up in the body and cause damage to the nervous system. _____ _____

19. Lung cancer, emphysema, and heart disease are ailments often linked to air pollution. _____ _____

20. The effects of air pollution usually develop slowly and manifest themselves only after many years. _____ _____

21. Sometimes, however, we see the immediate effects of air pollution. _____ _____

22. Belgium's Meuse River Valley, London, and Donora, Pennsylvania, were sites of major air pollution disasters. _____ _____

23. In Donora during October 1948 almost one-half of the town's inhabitants became ill from air pollution. _____ _____

24. Even worse, there were twenty deaths as a result of stagnant, polluted air. _____ _____

25. A five-day smog in London during 1952 hospitalized thousands and killed four thousand. _____ _____

NAME _____ SCORE _____

DIRECTIONS   In the following sentences underline the subject once, the verb twice, and the direct object of the verb (if any) three times. Then enter subject, verb, and object in the blanks below the sentences.

EXAMPLE   *Subject*   *Verb*   *Object*
Air pollution costs money and lives.
                                                                    money
            _____pollution_____   _____costs_____   _____lives_____

1. Experts attribute many financial expenditures to air pollution.

    _____ _____ _____

2. One immediately thinks of disability payments to victims of respiratory ailments.

    _____ _____ _____

3. The average person, however, overlooks other financial losses.

    _____ _____ _____

4. These losses include diseased livestock, ruined crops, and discolored and corroded products.

    _____ _____ _____

5. Have you seen any deterioration around your own home as a result of air pollution?

    _____ _____ _____

6. One finds classic examples of air pollution damage in Italy.

    _____ _____ _____

7. Sculpture has been standing in the squares of Rome and Florence for hundreds of years.

    _____ _____ _____

8. Now pollution is destroying these treasured works of art.

    _____ _____ _____

9. Americans, like Europeans, must constantly clean, repair, and replace articles affected by air pollution.

    _____ _____ _____

10. White as a color may disappear.

           _____   _____   _____

11. Can you imagine a white house in a smog-shrouded area?

           _____   _____   _____

12. What estimate would you give for the cost of air pollution?

           _____   _____   _____

13. The estimates of experts, of course, vary.

           _____   _____   _____

14. One estimate sets a conservative figure of five hundred dollars per year for each family.

           _____   _____   _____

15. Unhappily, most pollution experts see worse times ahead.

           _____   _____   _____

16. Many pessimistically predict gas masks and domed cities as our only hope.

           _____   _____   _____

17. In Japan many people have already purchased and used gas masks.

           _____   _____   _____

18. The prospect of wearing a gas mask does not appeal to anyone.

           _____   _____   _____

19. But survival may dictate the use of such a device.

           _____   _____   _____

20. What kind of paraphernalia will we be using in the year 2000 just to breathe?

           _____   _____   _____

Subject and verb in compound sentences

Exercise 1-4

NAME _____ SCORE _____

DIRECTIONS Insert an inverted caret (V) between main clauses in the following compound sentences. Then enter in the blanks at the right the subject and verb of each main clause. Note that the clauses are correctly joined either (1) by a comma plus *and, but, or, nor,* or *for,* or (2) by a semicolon.

	Subject	*Verb*
EXAMPLE There are many adverse results of air pollution;^V one of these is a more frightening possibility than any other.	*results* *one*	*are* *is*

1. Ecologists do not agree about what effects air pollution has on the earth's climate, but they do agree that the effects can be disastrous.

2. Air pollution screens out many of the sun's rays; thus the earth's surface becomes cooler.

3. The earth's temperature has dropped since 1940, and many ecologists predict that air pollution will cause another ice age.

4. Some ecologists theorize that the earth's climate will eventually be too cold to support life; others foresee quite a different end for life.

5. The burning of fossil and nuclear fuels heats up the atmosphere; thus our climate could become too hot to support life.

6. Another effect of overheating the atmosphere is flooding, for the great polar ice caps could melt and raise the water level above the elevation of many of our land areas.

7. These two theories remind one of

Robert Frost's poem "Fire and Ice";
the poem speculates about the cause
of our destruction.

_____

8. Frost says that what he knows about
desire makes him favor fire as the
earth's end; yet he also finds ice a
logical doom because of the hatred
in the world.

9. There is still another speculation
about the earth's final end; it is perhaps the most frightening of all and
the easiest to comprehend.

10. The burning of fossil fuels increases
the amount of carbon dioxide in the
air; therefore more plant life is required to use up the carbon dioxide
and to produce oxygen.

11. Ecologists fear that man may destroy
most of his plant life through pollution and urban development; then
there would be no oxygen.

12. In addition, without a proper oxygen
supply man is vulnerable to destruction in another way, for oxygen prevents the ultraviolet rays of the sun
from burning up the earth.

13. One cannot feel comfortable knowing that the carbon dioxide level in
the atmosphere is rising, nor is he
happy to look out at the smog surrounding his cities.

14. Man wants an instant, easy cure for
air pollution, but no such cure is
possible.

Subordinate (dependent) clauses

NAME _____ SCORE _____

DIRECTIONS   Classify each italicized subordinate clause in the following sentences as an adjective (*adj*), an adverb (*adv*), or a noun (*n*). If you need further practice in identifying subjects and verbs, underline each subject once and each verb twice. Notice the words that introduce the various clauses.

EXAMPLE

Clause

Everyone agrees *that air pollution is undesirable.*   ___*n*___

1. People are uncertain about *what steps should be taken to decrease or eliminate air pollution.*   _____

2. In recent years industries *that pollute the atmosphere* have been subject to prosecution.   _____

3. *After they have been given notice to control their atmospheric emission,* the polluting industries must often be fined for failure to comply.   _____

4. At one time the government was ready to prosecute four major automobile companies *because they delayed the installation of antipollution devices.*   _____

5. The suit was dropped *when the companies agreed to proceed with the development and installation of such devices.*   _____

6. The automobile industry claims *that it can eventually produce a pollution-free internal combustion engine.*   _____

7. *That it can or will do so* many critics of the industry doubt.   _____

8. These critics recommend *that we turn to a different power source for cars.*   _____

9. The President has drafted a plan *that will make "unconventional" cars available during the 1970's or 1980's.*   _____

10. People *who work on the designs of these cars* are considering steam engines, gas turbines, and electricity as power sources.   _____

11. The desire for clean air is also reflected in the amount of money *the federal government spends on air pollution control.*   _____

12. Federal spending rose from $12.7 million in 1963 to $45.5 million in 1969, a rate of increase *that is expected to continue during the 1970's.*   _____

13. It is also significant *that President Nixon's first official act was to sign a bill creating the Council on Environmental Control.* _____

14. There are still other signs *which point to our growing concern for clean air.* _____

15. The United Nations, *which has long been concerned about world peace,* is now actively involved in the effort to improve the world's environment. _____

16. In May 1972 representatives from all over the world met in Stockholm to consider *what can be done to save our environment.* _____

17. Maurice Strong, *who has been named Secretary General of the United Nations Conference on the Human Environment,* has the enthusiastic support of the United States in his efforts to organize the global conference. _____

18. Strong insists *that the environment is "the most international of all the great issues facing the world today."* _____

19. *Since the environment is a universal concern,* the nations of the world have a reason to cooperate with one another. _____

20. The 1970's are the years *when man will determine the future of his environment.* _____

NAME _____ SCORE _____

DIRECTIONS   Bracket the subordinate clauses in the following sentences. Then in the blanks at the right classify each clause as an adjective (*adj*), an adverb (*adv*), or a noun (*n*) and write out the first word of the clause. If you need further practice in identifying subjects and verbs, underscore each subject once and each verb twice.

EXAMPLE   *Clause*

[If progress is to be made in the fight against
   air pollution,] we must find ways to dis-
   courage the polluters.   *adv*   *If*

1. Laurence I. Moss, who speaks for the
   Sierra Club and other environmentalist
   groups, urges the taxation of polluters.   _____   _____

2. Environmentalists once argued that taxation was not the solution.   _____   _____

3. But most who formerly opposed this approach now see it as the only feasible
   course to be followed.   _____   _____

4. The system they suggest is fairly simple. _____   _____

5. When an industry is found to be polluting
   the air, it is fined or taxed a certain amount
   for each pound of pollution emitted.   _____   _____

6. Power plants, which emit 60 percent of all
   the sulfur oxides, contribute more than
   any other single industry to air pollution. _____   _____

7. Yet it is obvious that the government cannot shut down our sources of electrical
   power.   _____   _____

8. What the government might do is tax the
   power plants for their emissions.   _____   _____

9. Power companies, as well as other polluting industries, would be encouraged to
   develop the technology that would eliminate or at least limit their emissions.   _____   _____

10. Because tax payments would be as expensive as developing methods to control emissions, industries would be encouraged to spend money on research. _____ _____

11. One outcome of this plan is apparent to anyone who thinks about it. _____ _____

12. The public, whose cause is being served, must also be willing to pay higher electric bills to cover the cost of research. _____ _____

13. This cost is still cheaper than what is now being spent to pay for the health and property damage from air pollution. _____ _____

14. Cleaner air to breathe should be worth whatever the cost for research might be. _____ _____

15. Another incentive to reduce air pollution is being tried in Boston, where traffic contributes an excessive amount of carbon monoxide and nitrogen oxides to the air. _____ _____

16. Most of the thirty-three thousand automobiles which enter Boston between seven and nine o'clock each morning carry only one commuter. _____ _____

17. The Prudential Life Insurance Company, whose goal is to reduce the number of automobiles with single occupants, offers a special incentive to car pools. _____ _____

18. If a car carries three or more persons, it is eligible for free parking in the company's garage. _____ _____

19. Those who choose to travel alone face a parking fee of as much as forty dollars a month in a commercial garage. _____ _____

20. Thus whenever they can, workers at the Prudential Company prefer to share a ride. _____ _____

NAME _____ SCORE _____

DIRECTIONS   In the following sentences classify each italicized phrase as a noun (*n*), a verb (*v*), or a modifier (*mod*). Remember that a phrase used as a modifier may function as either an adjective or an adverb. (You may want to practice identifying the noun and modifying phrases as prepositional phrases, infinitive phrases, participial phrases, or gerund phrases.)

EXAMPLE   *Phrase*

The airplane, as well as the automobile, emits hydrocarbons *into the atmosphere*.   *mod*

1. At New York's La Guardia and Kennedy airports, the air is heavily polluted *with hydrocarbons*.   _____

2. In fact, Kennedy Airport *can be labeled* one of the most heavily polluted areas in our country.   _____

3. It is not unusual *to see fifteen or twenty airplanes* lined up for takeoff.   _____

4. The exhaust *coming from a jet engine* is directed toward the next plane in line for takeoff.   _____

5. The exhaust fumes enter the ventilating system *of the plane*.   _____

6. *Breathing these fumes* adversely affects the passengers' respiratory systems.   _____

7. The passengers *afflicted with respiratory ailments* are, of course, more seriously affected than those who have no such afflictions.   _____

8. But the hydrocarbons from the exhausts of jet engines *do result* in irritation to all passengers' lungs.   _____

9. *To minimize the intake of exhaust fumes*, pilots point the noses of their airplanes away from the direct blasts of the engines ahead.   _____

10. This practice helps to reduce the hazards to airline passengers, but it obviously does not solve the problem of pollution *around airports*.   _____

11. There is one obvious way *to reduce the pollution* around airports.   _____

12. Only a few planes *should be allowed* to queue up at one time for takeoff.   _____

13. *Reducing the number of planes* spewing their exhaust fumes into the air would greatly reduce the pollution. _____

14. *To avoid excessive exhausts,* the New York City Task Force on Air Pollution has recommended that airlines and control authorities use a sensible system of lining up planes for takeoff. _____

15. Planes should be directed to remain at their gates with their engines off *until a few minutes* before takeoff time. _____

16. *Controlling airplane exhausts* is becoming a matter of serious concern to environmentalists. _____

17. More and more people are turning *to airplanes* for their transportation. _____

18. Thus the sky *is being filled* with more planes with bigger engines. _____

19. *While landing or taking off,* a jet plane produces as much pollution as seventy-two cars running full force for twenty minutes. _____

20. At a busy airport *like Chicago's O'Hare International* the daily pollution from planes is equivalent to the amount that would be produced by 47,220 cars. _____

NAME _____ SCORE _____

DIRECTIONS   Classify the following sentences as simple (S), compound (CD), complex (CX), or compound-complex (CC).

Type of
Sentence

EXAMPLE

The first major air pollution disaster in the United States occurred in Donora, Pennsylvania, in October 1948.   *S* _____

1. When one reads an eyewitness account of the Donora disaster, he can better understand how serious a matter air pollution is. _____

2. Donora, a town in western Pennsylvania, had a population of about twelve thousand in 1948. _____

3. On Wednesday, October 27, an autumn fog, which was denser and colder than the usual fog, rolled in off the Monongahela River, but no one paid any real attention to it. _____

4. Some people in the town were discussing the coming Presidential election; others were talking about the just completed baseball season. _____

5. Stan Musial, the town's native son, was a much more popular topic of conversation than was the increasing fog. _____

6. The weather report announced that a temperature inversion had occurred. _____

7. The temperature was dropping and fog was being trapped in the valley. _____

8. The fog included fumes from factories, from chimneys, from automobiles, and from passing boats and trains. _____

9. By Friday the citizens of Donora could not only see the smog but could also feel it and taste it. _____

10. The president of the Board of Health in Donora recalls that the air had a definite oily taste to it and that one got a queasy feeling in his stomach from breathing it. _____

11. The annual Halloween Parade marched down the main street, but the onlookers could hardly see it. _____

12. By ten o'clock Friday night so many citizens of Donora were ill that the hospitals in nearby communities were overcrowded. _____

13. A local funeral director said he spent all of Friday night and Saturday collecting the sick and the dead. _____

14. Because of the blackness of the smog, he often had to lead the ambulance on foot. _____

15. Finding it almost impossible to breathe, the people panicked. _____

16. Many who tried to sleep propped themselves against chairs because they could not breathe lying down. _____

17. By Sunday rain and wind had dispersed the smog, but not before the country had witnessed its first major air pollution disaster. _____

18. Twenty people in Donora died and 5,910 became ill. _____

19. Those who had histories of respiratory illness were, of course, more severely affected than those who did not; still, four of the dead had no previous record of respiratory disease. _____

20. In 1948 few people were concerned about air pollution, but the citizens of Donora were forced to think about it. _____

21. No one who was living in Donora at that time can forget the five days when the smog was so thick one could taste it. _____

22. Yet, surprisingly enough, the communities in the area did not adopt air pollution codes as a result of the disaster. _____

23. In 1948 it was very unpopular to fight against air pollution, since dirty skies were thought to be indicative of progress. _____

24. Mill workers were afraid that their source of income would be closed down if they opposed air pollution. _____

25. This same attitude persists today, but more and more people are concluding that air pollution must be stopped, whatever the cost might be. _____

Grammatical types of sentence

NAME _____ SCORE _____

DIRECTIONS   Classify the following sentences as simple (*S*), compound (*CD*), complex (*CX*), or compound-complex (*CC*).

Type of
Sentence

EXAMPLE

There has been a significant change in public opinion about air pollution since the Donora disaster of 1948.

S

1. Although public opinion about air pollution has changed, we have only begun the struggle for clean air.

2. The second annual report of the Council on Environmental Quality concludes that air pollution in general has increased since 1969.

3. In a few areas, at least, some progress has been made.

4. Air pollution from the internal combustion engine has declined slightly as newer cars with antipollution devices have replaced older cars without them.

5. There has also been a slight decline in pollution from solid wastes, perhaps because municipal dumps now do less open-air burning than they did in the past.

6. The overall picture of the state of our air is not good, though, especially in the inner cities, where business and industry tend to be concentrated.

7. New York, Chicago, Los Angeles, and Philadelphia lead the country in population, and they also lead in air pollution.

8. One obvious difficulty in controlling air pollution is the monitoring of the offenders.

9. It is often difficult to determine just where the air pollution is coming from and just how much pollution a given offender is producing.

10. Devices such as laser detection systems are now being developed to make the job of monitoring easier and more efficient.

11. There are some people, like Dr. Raymond Slavin, who feel that our approach to air pollution is backward.

12. Dr. Slavin questions the advisability of leaving a pollutant in the air until it is proved harmful.

13. The burden of proof should be reversed; that is, no one should be allowed to release any substance into the air until it is proved harmless. _____

14. This principle is used in the case of drugs and food additives, and Dr. Slavin recommends it for the control of our air. _____

15. After all, as he points out, the principle can be considered even more logical for air than for foods and drugs. _____

16. We have a wide range of choice in foods and drugs but little choice in air. _____

17. Certainly one thing to be cultivated in the fight against air pollution is greenery, since it gives off oxygen. _____

18. Grass alone on a small plot of ground, fifty by fifty feet, gives off enough oxygen to meet the needs of a family of four. _____

19. Because of the oxygen-producing ability of green things, it is not facetious to recommend the planting of even one tree. _____

20. We must preserve our parks and open spaces, and we must support the development of even more areas of greenery. _____

21. The Council on Environmental Quality recommends that cities build rapid-transit systems not only to eliminate traffic congestion and automobile exhausts but also to provide more space for trees and grass. _____

22. An asphalt campground is not a satisfactory substitute for a forest, and a concrete playground is quite different from a grassy field. _____

23. There are many approaches to air pollution, then, and no one of them is a cure-all. _____

24. People must work as individuals and in groups to control air pollution. _____

25. We do not want to witness a disappearance of blue skies, nor do we want to have to wear gas masks to survive. _____

Sentence Fragment frag 2

2

Do not carelessly write an ineffective sentence fragment—a phrase or a subordinate clause—as if it were a complete sentence.

People frequently use sentence fragments effectively in speech and sometimes in writing. Any telephone conversation clearly illustrates the use of sentence fragments that communicate the speaker's thoughts. Generally, though, in formal speeches and writing, complete sentences are used.

A sentence fragment is usually either a phrase or a subordinate clause detached from a main clause. To be complete, a sentence must contain at least one main clause. A sentence fragment may be corrected (1) by making it into a sentence or (2) by attaching it to a sentence or to a main clause.

PHRASE   Having only one tusk.   [Participial phrase]

SENTENCE   The elephant had only one tusk.   [Fragment made into a sentence]

SENTENCE   Having only one tusk, the elephant lost the fight.   [Fragment attached to a main clause]

SUBORDINATE CLAUSE   Because the elephant had only one tusk.   [Subordinate clause]

SENTENCE   The elephant had only one tusk.   [Fragment made into a sentence]

SENTENCE   Because the elephant had only one tusk, he lost the fight.   [Fragment attached to a main clause]

As you proofread your compositions, check for sentence fragments by asking yourself two questions: (1) Does each word group that is punctuated as a sentence have both a subject and a predicate? (2) If a clause is introduced by a subordinator or a relative pronoun, is a main or independent clause also included in the word group?

Comma Splice and Fused Sentence cs 3

3

Do not carelessly link two main clauses (sentences) with only a comma between them (comma splice) or run main clauses together without any punctuation (fused sentence).

COMMA SPLICE   The newly married couple needed to save money, they built their own beach house.   [Two main clauses linked by only a comma]

25

FUSED SENTENCE   The newly married couple needed to save money they built their own beach house. [Two main clauses run together with no punctuation]

Often the best way to correct the comma splice or fused sentence is to subordinate one of the main clauses.

REVISION 1   Because the newly married couple needed to save money, they built their own beach house.

PATTERN   **SUBORDINATE CLAUSE, MAIN CLAUSE.**

The subordinate clause, of course, may follow the main clause, in which case there is usually no need for the comma.

The newly married couple built their own beach house because they needed to save money.

PATTERN   **MAIN CLAUSE   SUBORDINATE CLAUSE.**

There are several other methods of correction.

REVISION 2   The newly married couple needed to save money. They built their own beach house.

PATTERN   **SENTENCE. SENTENCE.**

REVISION 3   The newly married couple had little money, but they wanted their own beach house.

PATTERN   **MAIN CLAUSE,** *coordinating conjunction* **MAIN CLAUSE.**

REVISION 4   The newly married couple needed to save money; they built their own beach house.

PATTERN   **MAIN CLAUSE; MAIN CLAUSE.**

Caution: Whenever a conjunctive adverb (such as *however, therefore*), a transitional phrase (such as *for example, in fact*), or a direct quotation is used, one must be especially careful to avoid the comma splice or fused sentence.

COMMA SPLICE   The newly married couple needed to save money, therefore they built their own beach house.

REVISED   The newly married couple needed to save money; therefore they built their own beach house.

FUSED SENTENCE   The newly married couple showed their versatility in many ways for example they built their own beach house.

REVISED   The newly married couple showed their versatility in many ways; for example, they built their own beach house.

COMMA SPLICE   "Many people have lost the ability to do things with their hands," the couple said, "we want to preserve that ability."

REVISED   "Many people have lost the ability to do things with their hands," the couple said. "We want to preserve that ability."

While comma splices and fused sentences sometimes appear in fiction and even in essays, the inexperienced writer will do well to make sure that main clauses in a sentence are separated (1) by a comma plus a coordinating conjunction or (2) by a semicolon.

Verbs distinguished from verbals; sentence fragments   Exercise 2-1

NAME _____ SCORE _____

DIRECTIONS   In the following word groups underline each subject with one straight line, each verbal with one wavy line, and each verb with two straight lines. Then enter each subject and verb in the blanks at the right. If a word group contains no true subject and verb, indicate a sentence fragment by writing *frag* in the blank for the verb. Some fragments have neither subjects nor verbs.

EXAMPLE

	Subject	*Verb*
Our water, like our air, having been taken for granted.	*water*	*frag*

1. Water being in seemingly endless supply. _____ _____

2. The water was wasted and poisoned by man. _____ _____

3. People are now forced to recognize the damage they have done. _____ _____

4. Thousands of fish floating on the water. _____ _____

5. Oil slicks having been sighted even in the middle of the ocean. _____ _____

6. Once safe drinking water now polluted with chemicals and dangerous bacteria. _____ _____

7. Little clean water remains. _____ _____

8. Once beautiful Lake Erie now resembles a cesspool. _____ _____

9. Lake Michigan doomed to die in twenty years. _____ _____

10. After investigating the various bodies of water in the state, the Illinois Department of Public Health declared all rivers and streams too polluted for safe swimming. _____ _____

	Subject	Verb

11. Many other states facing the same bleak situation with regard to their waterways. _____ _____

12. More frightening still, even some of our oceans appear to be dying. _____ _____

13. The Gulf of Mexico often mentioned as a candidate for early doom. _____ _____

14. Each year more and more areas of the Gulf becoming contaminated with human, industrial, and agricultural wastes. _____ _____

15. To get relatively uncontaminated fish and shrimp, fishing boats must go farther out to sea each year. _____ _____

16. Assuming that pollution continues at the present rate, there will eventually be no safe fishing areas left. _____ _____

17. One of the horrifying accounts of water pollution received from Thor Heyerdahl during his crossing of the Atlantic on *Ra 2*. _____ _____

18. Floating lumps of solidified asphaltlike oil stretching for at least fourteen hundred miles into the open Atlantic waters. _____ _____

19. Although normally requiring thousands of years to die from natural causes. _____ _____

20. Given man's help, a lake may lose its aquatic life in twenty to forty years. _____ _____

NAME _____ SCORE _____

DIRECTIONS   Identify each fragment by writing *frag* in the blank at the right, and each sentence by writing *C*. Revise each fragment either by attaching it to a main clause or by making it into a sentence of its own.

EXAMPLES

Our coastlines are deteriorating,   *C*

Because of landfill projects and pollution.   *frag*

are
Marshlands gradually disappearing.   *frag*

1. When we read that 73 percent of our nation's coasts have been modified. _____

2. We may be astounded. _____

3. But the Department of the Interior reports that almost three-fourths of our coastlines have sustained moderate to severe modifications. _____

4. Urban development accounting for much of the change. _____

5. Marshlands are filled in so that houses can be built. _____

6. A great number of people who live along our country's coastlines. _____

7. Almost three-fourths of our country's population is concentrated there. _____

8. And nine of the nation's largest cities are built on the coasts. _____

9. Between 1950 and 1969 dredging and filling accounting for the loss of approximately 650,000 acres of marshland. _____

10. The despoliation is continuing. _____

11. The interaction of the land and sea which is changed by dredging and filling. _____

12. The low areas formerly having acted as habitats for many species of animal life and as protection against floods and high winds. _____

13. As a result of their disappearance many unpleasant repercussions are experienced. _____

14. For example, the elimination of rest stops for migratory birds. _____

15. Along with urbanization and industrialization of the coastlines has come pollution. _____

16. More than one-fourth of the areas inhabited by shellfish now polluted. _____

17. The more populated the coastline area, the more pollutants are dumped into the water. _____

18. The coastlines of New York and New Jersey being the most populated. _____

19. Pollution is extremely serious in these areas. _____

20. With 40 percent of the bottom of New York Harbor covered with sludge. _____

21. Runoff from sewage continues. _____

22. Included in the list of other threatened areas are the Chesapeake Bay, the San Francisco Bay, and the Florida and Texas coasts. _____

23. Although the West Coast has fared better than the East Coast. _____

24. There are signs of increasing deterioration. _____

25. Such as oil-stained beaches and more marinas and houses built on land-filled areas. _____

NAME _____ SCORE _____

DIRECTIONS   The following word groups show that a sentence fragment is often placed before or after a closely related complete thought. First identify each complete sentence by writing *C* in the numbered blank at the right, and each sentence fragment by writing *frag*. Then complete each fragment (1) by rewriting it to form a sentence by itself or (2) by attaching the fragment to the complete sentence. If you consider some other method of correction preferable, be prepared to point it out.

EXAMPLES

¹The threat of extinction hangs over all of our waterways, –   1.____C____

²Over our oceans as well as our rivers and lakes.   2.___frag___

¹Famous for his undersea explorations. ²Jacques Cousteau   1._____
estimates that marine life has decreased by 40 percent in   2._____
the last twenty years. ³Is Cousteau correct? ⁴No one can say   3._____
for certain. ⁵Because no measurement of ocean life was   4._____
made twenty years ago. ⁶And none is being made today.   5._____

⁷Many ecologists feel that Cousteau has not overestimated   6._____
the damage. ⁸Considering the frightening facts about pollu-   7._____
tion of the seas that have been recorded. ⁹Such as the rapid   8._____
disappearance of haddock and yellowtail flounder off our   9._____
northeastern coast. ¹⁰In one of the most horrifying accounts   10._____
of pollution recorded. ¹¹Forty-nine persons in Japan died   11._____
when they ate fish that had been poisoned with industrial
mercury.

¹²Although what happened in Japan sounds like science   12._____
fiction. ¹³It could occur elsewhere in the world. ¹⁴Shellfish 13._____
beds off the Georgia and Texas coasts have been closed.   14._____
¹⁵As a result of mercury contamination. ¹⁶According to   15._____
the director of the World Life Research Institute. ¹⁷The   16._____
buildup of toxic substances in the waters around industrial-   17._____
ized areas "has reached frightening proportions."

¹⁸In addition to mercury contamination. ¹⁹Many other pollutants are present in our waterways. ²⁰For example, DDT. ²¹Which has killed innumerable shrimp off the Texas coast. ²²And has disturbed the reproduction cycle of the speckled trout.

²³The figures on our disposal of wastes into the sea are staggering. ²⁴In 1968 alone the United States dumping forty-nine million tons of wastes into the sea. ²⁵Including thirteen million tons of pollutants. ²⁶The results are predictable. ²⁷But when we read that hardly a living thing survives within a twenty-mile area off the coast of New York. ²⁸We are still surprised.

²⁹We must remember that every chemical man discards finds its way to the sea. ³⁰Unless it is buried under special conditions. ³¹Chemicals then collect in plankton. ³²Which is the major source of food for small fish.

³³Having already ingested some of the toxic chemicals in the sea. ³⁴Small fish further increase the store of poisons in their bodies when they feed on the contaminated plankton. ³⁵Large fish, of course, eating the small fish. ³⁶The concentration of chemicals in their livers is multiplied. ³⁷Thus the toxic chemicals work their way up the food chain. ³⁸Eventually winding up on man's dinner plate. ³⁹Since the fertilizers used to grow feed usually come from the sea. ⁴⁰Chicken and beef, as well as fish, may become contaminated.

18._____

19._____

20._____

21._____

22._____

23._____

24._____

25._____

26._____

27._____

28._____

29._____

30._____

31._____

32._____

33._____

34._____

35._____

36._____

37._____

38._____

39._____

40._____

Comma splices and fused sentences

NAME _____ SCORE _____

DIRECTIONS In each of the following sentences insert an inverted caret (V) between main clauses where a comma splice might occur. Then indicate in the first blank at the right whether the sentence is correct (*C*), contains a comma splice (*CS*), or is fused (*F*). Correct each error by the best method, showing in the second blank whether you have used subordination (*sub*), a period (**.**) a semicolon (**;**), or a comma plus a coordinating conjunction (*conj*).

EXAMPLES

Jacques Cousteau has a solution to the problem of
    chemical pollution of our oceans, it will require
    a great deal of money.   *CS*   *conj*

Cousteau is not optimistic; he feels man will close
    his eyes to the problem of water pollution.   *F*   **;**

1. Cousteau recommends that we extract toxic chemicals from our waterways, then pack them in watertight containers.   _____   _____

2. The containers must be stored beneath the water level, otherwise, the toxic materials will return to our oceans.   _____   _____

3. Cousteau recommends salt mines for a storage place they are not a part of the water cycle.   _____   _____

4. We know that salt mines are not a part of the water cycle, they have been dry for millions of years.   _____   _____

5. Storing our chemical wastes in salt mines, then, would prevent them from entering our oceans.   _____   _____

6. The cost of such a procedure will be high everything we buy will increase in price.   _____   _____

7. The cost of not doing anything about chemical wastes will be higher still, Cousteau foresees man's disappearance from the earth if he continues to pollute the oceans.   _____ _____

8. We will disappear, Cousteau feels, insects will replace us.   _____ _____

9. We can still save our seas, however, we must change our attitude toward the life found there.   _____ _____

10. Cousteau notes that primitive man was first a nomadic hunter then he learned to farm.   _____ _____

11. Cousteau thinks that we must take this same step in our approach to the life of the sea, namely, we must learn to farm it rather than hunt in it.   _____ _____

12. At present we are barbaric in our treatment of the life of the sea, we will become civilized when we look upon the sea as the farmer looks upon his land.   _____ _____

13. For many years ignorance has been the excuse for our conduct toward the sea now we can no longer use ignorance as an excuse.   _____ _____

14. If we do not change our conduct, greed is our only excuse, according to Cousteau.   _____ _____

15. Cousteau is a soft-spoken man yet the words he speaks are not easy to bear.   _____ _____

16. Other ecologists are equally forthright in their message to man, for example, Wesley Marx

NAME _____ SCORE _____

warns us about the fate of our oceans in his

book *The Frail Ocean.*   _____   _____

17. Man has always felt that even if the land disap-

peared, the ocean would still be there, clean

and pure.   _____   _____

18. "The concept of an all-powerful ocean is today

obsolete," Marx warns, "the ocean can no longer

take care of itself."   _____   _____

19. When a forest dies, everyone can see the evi-

dence, when an ocean dies, the signs are often

invisible.   _____   _____.

20. Man still sees blue water and big waves conse-

quently, he assumes that all is well with the

sea.   _____   _____

21. In the last few years, however, we have been

able to see some obvious signs of destruction,

for example, oil slicks have spread to beaches in

various states.   _____   _____

22. A lady in California kept a daily journal of the

Santa Barbara oil slick, one of the worst to

spread to the United States coastlines.   _____   _____

23. The oil slick eventually covered the entire Santa

Barbara Cove, killing most of the birds and fish

in its path.   _____   _____

24. The citizens of the coastal area tried desperately to save the birds of the area, still, few survived the ordeal of having their wings and beaks covered with oil. _____ _____

25. Various cleanup solutions were tried nothing worked better than the primitive method of spreading straw along the beaches to soak up the oil as it drifted ashore. _____ _____

NAME _____ SCORE _____

DIRECTIONS   Classify each of the following as a fragmentary sentence (*frag*), a comma splice (*CS*), or a correct sentence (*C*). Revise each faulty sentence.

EXAMPLE

One of the most recent kinds of pollution to be discussed ~~being~~ *is*
   thermal pollution.   *frag*

1. Our consumption of electrical power having doubled every
   ten years.   _____

2. To meet the need for more electricity, power companies
   have been building larger generating plants, many of them
   nuclear-powered.   _____

3. The waste heat that power companies produce must be got-
   ten rid of, it usually goes into a nearby river.   _____

4. The water that is drained out of the rivers for use by the
   power companies is cold, however, the water that is re-
   turned to the rivers is warm.   _____

5. Although some species of fish can stand an increase in water
   temperature, even a slight warming of the river will kill many
   game fish.   _____

6. The rise in temperature also depletes some of the oxygen in
   the water, thus the river may not be able to cleanse itself.   _____

7. Furthermore, the warmer water promotes the growth of blue-
   green algae, which use even more of the river's oxygen
   supply.   _____

8. The oxygen-depleted water, which eventually smells bad and
   tastes bad.   _____

9. No dirt may be added to the water, but the warmer temperature activates the sewage and other pollution that is
   already in the water.   _____

10. Thermal pollution is receiving a great deal of attention from ecologists, they believe that something can be done about it before the problem is too severe. _____

11. The technology for preventing thermal pollution is available, they claim, but as usual the technology costs money. _____

12. So far the most widely used method for cooling the water produced by generating plants is the cooling tower, a tall structure that allows the water to cool itself as it trickles down through air. _____

13. The cost of installation is the main objection raised against cooling towers, the price of generating power increasing about 5 percent when they are used. _____

14. The cost to the consumer being about 1 percent, or five dollars per year. _____

15. The main difficulty in the prevention of thermal pollution is that no one is in charge of this aspect of power plants, consequently, little is being done. _____

16. There are standards for the purity of river and lake water, but these standards apply to pollution caused by sewage and industrial wastes. _____

17. Thermal pollution has come upon us suddenly, unfortunately it will not leave us suddenly. _____

18. Since the demand for electrical power continues to increase each year and more and more million-kilowatt plants are being built to satisfy the demand. _____

19. Some states are taking action against thermal pollution, for example, Vermont has prevented an atomic power plant from raising the temperature of the Connecticut River by twenty degrees. _____

20. In addition to Vermont, Oregon and Washington have acted upon an "anti-degradation clause," which stipulates that no river or lake can be made worse than it now is. _____

NAME _____ SCORE _____

DIRECTIONS　Classify each of the following as a fragmentary sentence (*frag*), a comma splice (*CS*), or a correct sentence (*C*). Revise each faulty sentence.

EXAMPLE

Efforts are being made to halt water pollution;/however, there is no simple solution to the problem.

CS

1. In 1970 the President outlined a program for fighting water pollution, it included, among other things, the establishment of uniform standards for clean water.　　　_____

2. The program provides stricter penalties for industrial and municipal polluters, as much as ten thousand dollars a day for violators.　　　_____

3. Also included in the program are federal funds for improving municipal waste-treatment facilities.　　　_____

4. The solution to the problem of water pollution will not come overnight, in fact, the Secretary of the Interior estimates that even with our best efforts, at least five to seven years will be required to clean up our water.　　　_____

5. Others contending that it will take much longer than the Secretary of the Interior suggests.　　　_____

6. One source of water pollution in particular illustrates the complexity of the problem we face, the pollution resulting from phosphates in detergents.　　　_____

7. The addition of phosphates increases the cleaning power of detergents, at the same time the phosphates increase the degree of water pollution.　　　_____

8. Phosphates feed the algae and other plant life, which then flourish too well and upset the delicate balance of living things in water.　　　_____

9. The oxygen supply is quickly depleted, then eutrophication, or the death of a body of water, begins. _____

10. Many soap manufacturers having substituted other chemicals for phosphates and several states and cities having banned phosphate-bearing detergents. _____

11. In September 1971 the Surgeon General made a surprise announcement. _____

12. "My advice to the housewife at this time," he said, "is to use a phosphate detergent." _____

13. "Why are phosphates now recommended," many people asked, "they are obvious contributors to our pollution problem." _____

14. Studies have shown that chemicals substituted for phosphates present certain dangers, such as irritation to the eyes and nose. _____

15. One phosphate substitute was found to combine with other chemicals in drinking water, such as cadmium and mercury, thus producing a compound that caused birth defects in animals. _____

16. Because there does seem to be a health risk involved in the use of phosphate-substitute detergents. _____

17. Officials urged the building of new sewage plants and the modification of many existing ones to filter out the phosphates. _____

18. Some people who disagreed with the decision to return to phosphates. _____

19. Some states, counties, and cities maintaining the ban they had set on phosphates. _____

20. The phosphate dilemma is another illustration of the complexity of the water pollution problem, a problem that must nevertheless be dealt with. _____

4

Distinguish between adjectives and adverbs and use the appropriate forms.

Adjectives (in *italics* below) and adverbs (in **boldface** below) are modifiers. That is, they qualify or limit, make clearer or more specific, other words in the sentence. Any word modifying a noun or noun substitute is an adjective: *rapid* stream, *joyful* ringing of the bells. Any word modifying a verb, a participle, an infinitive, an adjective, another adverb, or even a whole clause is an adverb: flow **rapidly**; a **rapidly** *flowing* stream; a **very rapidly** *flowing* stream; **indeed,** the stream flows **rapidly**.

Forms of Adjectives and Adverbs

Both adjectives and adverbs usually have comparative forms: quick, quick*er,* quick*est;* quickly, **more** quickly, **most** quickly.

The *-ly* suffix nearly always makes adjectives into adverbs (*rapid,* **rapidly**; *joyful,* **joyfully**) and usually converts nouns into adjectives (friend, *friendly;* saint, *saintly*). Other suffixes that commonly make nouns into adjectives are *-al* (nation, *national*), *-ful* (hope, *hopeful*), *-ish* (boy, *boyish*), *-like* (life, *lifelike*), and *-ous* (danger, *dangerous*).

A few words ending in *-ly* (such as *only, early, cowardly*) may be either adjectives or adverbs, and the same is true for a considerable number of common words not ending in *-ly* (such as *far,* **far**; *fast,* **fast**; *late,* **late**; *little,* **little**).

Your dictionary shows the proper form for adjective and adverb, but you can know which form is needed only by determining the word modified.

4a   Use adverb forms as modifiers of verbs, adjectives, and other adverbs.

Especially common is the misuse of the adjective to modify a verb or verbal.

> NONSTANDARD   Can one love as easy as one can hate?   [Adjective *easy* misused as a modifier of the verb *can love*]
>
> STANDARD   Can one love as **easily** as one can hate?
>
> NONSTANDARD   My mother sure makes good pizza.   [*Sure* misused as a modifier of *makes*]
>
> STANDARD   My mother **surely** makes good pizza.

Another frequent error is the misuse of an adjective to modify another adjective.

> NONSTANDARD   An accountant makes a real good salary.   [Adjective *real* misused as a modifier of the other adjective *good*]

STANDARD	An accountant makes a **really** good salary.
NONSTANDARD	This is a relative untapped market. [*Relative* misused as a modifier of *untapped*]
STANDARD	This is a **relatively** untapped market.

4b Use adjectives rather than adverbs as subject complements.

As subject complements, adjectives always modify the subject. They usually follow but sometimes precede the verbs that link them with their subjects: *be, am, are, is, was, were, been, seen,* and *become* (and their equivalents) and *feel, taste, look, smell,* and *sound.*

PATTERN   SUBJECT—LINKING VERB—SUBJECT COMPLEMENT.
The rose smells *sweet.*   [*Sweet* rose]
Soft are the rose's petals.   [*Soft* petals]

Exception: The modifier should be an adverb when it refers to the action of the verb. In such a case the verb is not used as a linking verb.

PATTERN   SUBJECT—VERB—ADVERB.
The archeologist looked **expectantly** at the cave drawings.   [The adverb **expectantly** qualifies the verb *looked.*]
The chef **suspiciously** tasted the strange mixture.   [**Suspiciously** qualifies *tasted.*]

Note: A modifier following a verb and its direct object is an adjective when it refers to the object rather than to the action of the verb.

PATTERN   SUBJECT—VERB—OBJECT—OBJECT COMPLEMENT.
The engineer made the boiler *airtight.*   [*Airtight* is an adjective: *airtight* boiler.]
The boy held his shoulders *straight.*   [*Straight* shoulders]

4c Use appropriate forms for the comparative and the superlative.

| COMPARATIVE | Sophocles was the *better* of the two playwrights.   [Used to compare two things: the suffix *-er* or the adverb **more,** as in *more beautiful,* is the usual sign of the comparative.] |
| SUPERLATIVE | Today Sophocles is the *most famous* of the Greek playwrights.   [Commonly used to compare three or more things: the suffix *-est,* as in *wisest,* or the adverb **most** is the usual sign of the superlative.] |

4d Avoid any awkward or ambiguous use of a noun form as an adjective.

Although many noun forms (*house* trailer, *boat* dock, *television* show) are used effectively as adjectives, especially when appropriate adjectives are not available, such forms should be avoided when they are either awkward or ambiguous.

| AWKWARD | Education methods are changing. |
| BETTER | *Educational* methods are changing. |

Confusion of adjectives and adverbs

NAME _____ SCORE _____

DIRECTIONS   In each of the following sentences underline the word modified by the italicized word and indicate in the first blank at the right whether the italicized word is used as an adjective (*adj*) or an adverb (*adv*). In the second blank write *C* if the italicized word is the correct form for standard English; if not, supply the correct form.

EXAMPLES

Most <u>all</u> our land is eroded.   *adv*   *almost*

Many <u>areas</u> now look *bad*.   *adj*   *C*

1. Our land once appeared quite *differently* from what it is today.   _____   _____

2. North America was the *most richest blessed* of the continents.   _____   _____

3. The natural resources found here were *unbelievable* plentiful.   _____   _____

4. Great forests were *real* common.   _____   _____

5. And rich topsoil *surely* seemed inexhaustible.   _____   _____

6. But the pioneers took a *surprising* short time to deplete the forests and the topsoil.   _____   _____

7. As they moved *relentlessly* westward, they cut down the forests and plowed the land.   _____   _____

8. What was once rich land soon became *barrenly*.   _____   _____

9. Rain carried away the topsoil almost *continuous*.   _____   _____

10. Americans took *approximate* two hundred years to destroy one-third of their topsoil.   _____   _____

11. Too *frequent* the rain carried away much of the exposed topsoil.   _____   _____

12. The wind seemed equally *severely* in its treatment of the unprotected topsoil. _____ _____

13. Of the two forces of erosion—wind and water—wind was the *most* dramatic. _____ _____

14. The sky often looked *black* because of dust storms. _____ _____

15. In 1930 a great dust storm swept *mercilessly* across the midwest. _____ _____

16. For a week the sky was *terrible* dark with clouds of dust. _____ _____

17. Five midwestern states were transformed into desert and steppe very *quick*. _____ _____

18. The *sociology* accounts of the effects of the great dust storm are extremely depressing. _____ _____

19. Many of Woody Guthrie's songs speak *poignantly* of this period in American history. _____ _____

20. The fruits of carelessness always taste *bitterly*. _____ _____

5

Use the proper case form to show the function of pronouns or nouns in sentences.

The case of a pronoun is the form it takes to show its function in the sentence as subject of a verb (subjective or nominative case), possessor (possessive case), or object of a verb, verbal, or preposition (objective case). Nouns and some indefinite pronouns (*anyone, someone, everyone*) have a distinctive case form only for the possessive (the *boy's* book, the *boys'* mother: see **15a**), but six of our common pronouns have distinctive forms in all three cases and must be used with care.

SUBJECTIVE	I	we	he, she	they	who
POSSESSIVE	my	our	his, her	their	whose
	(mine)	(ours)	(hers)	(theirs)	
OBJECTIVE	me	us	him, her	them	whom

Note: The personal pronouns *it* and *you* change form only to indicate the possessive—*its, your (yours)*.

5a   Take special care with pronouns in apposition and in compound constructions.

(1) An appositive takes the same case as the noun or pronoun with which it is in apposition.

> We—my sister and *I* (NOT *me*)—share a dormitory room.   [*I* is in the subjective case because it is in apposition with the subject *we*.]
> Let's *you* and *me* (NOT *I*) get an apartment.   ["Let *us*—you and *me*—get an apartment." *Me* and *us* are in the same case.]

Note: Do not let an appositive following a pronoun trick you into making a mistake with case: *We* girls enjoy cooking.

(2) Compound constructions

> My sister and *I* (NOT *me*) often disagree.   [*I* is a subject of the verb.]
> Abner invited both my sister and *me* (NOT *I*).   [*Me* is an object.]

Note: *Myself (himself, ourselves,* and so on) is not a substitute for *I* or *me* (*he, us,* and so on); it is a reflexive or intensive pronoun: I hit *myself;* I *myself* will go. Avoid the illiterate forms of reflexive pronouns—*hisself, theirselves.*

5b   Determine the case of each pronoun by its use in its own clause.

(1) Pronoun as subject of a clause

The subject of a clause always takes the subjective case, even when the whole clause is the object of a verb or a preposition.

I am impressed by *whoever* is able to write well. [*Whoever* is the subject of *is able. Whoever is able to write well* is the object of *by*.]

I envy *whoever* expresses himself well. [The complete clause *whoever expresses himself well*, not merely the pronoun *whoever*, is the object of *envy*.]

(2) Pronoun followed by a parenthetical *I think, he says*, etc.

Do not allow such parenthetical expressions as *I think, he says, we know* to trick you into changing the subjective *who (whoever, whosoever)* to *whom (whomever, whomsoever)*.

A judge of the Supreme Court must be a man *who* (NOT *whom*) people know is above reproach. [*Who* is the subject of *is*.]

Brandeis was a judge *who* (NOT *whom*) I believe was such a person. [Brandeis was a judge *who* was such a person.]

(3) Pronouns following *than* or *as*

A pronoun following *than* or *as* takes the subjective or objective case according to whether the pronoun is subject or object of an implied verb.

He is older than *I* (*am*).

He likes you as much as (he likes) *me*.

He likes you better than *I* (like you).

5c   In formal writing use *whom* for all objects.

For *whom* does he work? [Good usage, formal or informal, always requires the objective *whom* immediately following a preposition.]

Informal English tends to avoid the use of the objective *whom* unless it comes immediately after a preposition: *Who* does he work for?

5d   A pronoun immediately before a gerund (verbal noun) is usually in the possessive case.

His becoming a doctor pleased his parents.

My parents approved of *my* (*our, his, her, their*) joining the Peace Corps.

5e   Use the objective case for the subject, object, or complement of an infinitive.

She invited *me* to visit *her*. [*Me* is the subject and *her* the object of the infinitive *to visit; me to visit her* is the object of the verb *invited*.]

5f   Use the subjective case for the complement of the verb *be*.

PATTERN   SUBJECT—LINKING VERB *BE*—COMPLEMENT.

| That | may be | she. |
| It | was | they. |

Note: Informal usage accepts *It is me* (*It's me*).

Case of pronouns

NAME _____ SCORE _____

DIRECTIONS   In the following sentences cross out the incorrect form within parentheses and write the correct form in the blank at the right. After your answers have
been checked, read the sentences aloud several times to accustom your ear to the
correct pronoun.

EXAMPLE

It is time for (~~we~~, us) to think about our land.   *us*

1. (Whoever, Whomever) visits Europe is usually impressed by the people's respect for their land.   _____

2. Kevin and (I, me, myself) were given a trip to Europe
   when we graduated from college.   _____

3. Kevin was as fascinated by the landscape as (I, me).   _____

4. The neatness of the countryside amazed us—both (he
   and I, him and me).   _____

5. Europeans, to (who, whom) land has a special meaning,
   seem to cultivate each blade of grass.   _____

6. Europeans are more careful with their land than (we,
   us) because they have fewer open spaces.   _____

7. There are still uninhabited areas for (we, us) to enjoy.   _____

8. But the fast disappearance of our open spaces should
   be apparent to (whoever, whomever) looks around.   _____

9. One person from Holland (who, whom) Kevin and I
   met spoke of the Dutch effort to reclaim land from the
   sea.   _____

10. (Him, His) explaining Holland's centuries-old battle
    against the sea made us realize how valuable land is.   _____

11. Americans are a people (who, whom) I think too often
    take the land for granted.   _____

12. We—Kevin and (I, me)—admired the tidy Dutch.   _____

13. We became more careful with our land as a result of
    (us, our) traveling through Holland.   _____

14. We now feel that (whoever, whomever) owns property
    has a serious obligation.   _____

15. (Us, We) Americans must take care of our land.   _____

NAME _____ SCORE _____

DIRECTIONS   In the following sentences strike out each incorrectly used pronoun and enter the correct form in the blank at the right. Be prepared to state the reason for each correction you make. For each sentence containing no pronoun in the wrong case, write *C* in the blank at the right. After your answers have been checked, read the sentences aloud several times to accustom your ear to the correct pronoun.

EXAMPLE

A vital concern to Kevin and ~~I~~ is the rapid disappearance of our forests.   *me*

1. Man once considered the forests an obstacle to him settling down.   _____

2. Today you and me realize that our forests provide more than beauty for us.   _____

3. Ecologists whom have studied the vital role of the forests tell us that wooded areas are necessary for the stability of both soil and water.   _____

4. Whoever has seen a barren area where a forest once stood sees for hisself the effect the forest has on the topsoil.   _____

5. Our forests provide we Americans with our best soil cover.   _____

6. For we who carelessly destroy the forests, the reward is soil erosion and drought.   _____

7. An old Indian whom I read about made a frightening prediction.   _____

8. He said to us Americans: "Our country is a new Atlantis; one day it will disappear in the Ocean."   _____

9. The Indian was older than me.   _____

10. Perhaps when I have seen as much as him, I will fully understand his prediction.   _____

11. Americans are people whom everyone says are richly blessed.   _____

12. But blessings are maintained by those who appreciate them and use them well.   _____

13. Ecologists tell us—you and I—that the handwriting is already on the wall: the blessings are running out.   _____

14. Adlai Stevenson spoke of we as passengers on a little spaceship.   _____

15. It is us, he said, who must prevent the spacecraft from being annihilated.   _____

6

Make a verb agree in number with its subject; make a pronoun agree in number with its antecedent.

Singular subjects require singular verbs; plural subjects require plural verbs.[1] Pronouns agree with their antecedents (the words to which they refer) in the same way. Note that in the subject the *-s* ending is the sign of the plural while in the verb it is the sign of the third person singular.

> The true *strength* of a nation *is* hard to define.   [Singular subject—singular verb]
>
> The true *strengths* of a nation *are* hard to define.   [Plural subject—plural verb]
>
> The *boy* repairs *his* own car.   [Singular antecedent—singular pronoun]
>
> The *boys* repair *their* own cars.   [Plural antecedent—plural pronoun]

Single out each subject and its verb and connect them mentally: *strength is, strengths are.* Do the same with each antecedent and its pronoun: *boy ← his, boys ← their.* This practice will make it easy to avoid errors in agreement. If you find it difficult to distinguish verbs and relate them to their subjects, review **1a** and **1b**.

6a   Make a verb agree in number with its subject.

(1) Do not be misled by nouns or pronouns intervening between the subject and the verb or by subjects and verbs with endings difficult to pronounce.

> The *noise* of cars and motor boats *drowns out* (NOT *drown out*) the katydids.
> *Every one* of us *is* (NOT *are*) guilty of noise pollution.
> The *naturalist seeks* (NOT *seek*) a solution.

The number of the subject is not changed by the addition of parenthetical expressions introduced by such words as *with, together with, as well as, no less than, including, accompanied by.*

> *Amos,* together with Joe and David, *was immobilized* with fright.
> *Amos,* like his two brothers, *was* a skydiver.

(2) Subjects joined by *and* are usually plural.

> Our dog and a poodle *were* in the same cage.
> A retriever, a cocker spaniel, and a beagle *were housed* together.

Exceptions: A compound subject referring to a single person or to two or more things considered as a unit is singular.

---

[1] Although verbs do not have number, it is customary to use the terms *singular verb* for verbs with singular subjects and *plural verb* for those with plural subjects.

The quarterback and captain *was injured.* [A single individual was both quarterback and captain.]

Turkey and dressing *is* a popular dish at Thanksgiving. [Two nouns considered as a single entity]

Each or *every* preceding singular subjects joined by *and* calls for a singular verb.

Each counselor and each camper *has been advised* to wear shoes.
Every bramble and thorn *is* a menace to bare feet.

(3) Singular subjects joined by or, nor, either . . . or, neither . . . nor usually take a singular verb.

Neither the counselor nor the camper *is* very brave.
Either a frog or a cricket *is* probably *making* the noise.

When the meaning is felt to be plural, informal English occasionally uses the plural verb: "Neither she nor I *were dancing,* for we felt tired."

If one subject is singular and one plural, the verb usually agrees with the nearer subject.

Neither counselor nor campers *were invited.*
Neither campers nor counselor *was invited.*

Either the counselor or I *am* responsible.

Many writers prefer to recast such sentences and thus avoid the problem:

The invitation included neither counselor nor campers.
Either the counselor is responsible or I am. OR One of us is responsible.

(4) When the subject follows the verb (as in sentences beginning with there is, there are) special care is needed to determine the subject and to make sure that it agrees with the verb.

On the national scene, there *are* at least six *senators running* for the Presidency.
In our state there *is* only one *candidate* for governor.
There *are* few good *men* available.

Before a compound subject the first member of which is singular, a singular verb is sometimes used.

In one of the new buildings there *is* a *library,* which has no books, and a music *room* and six practice *rooms.*

Note: The expletive *it* is always followed by a singular verb: "It *is* the Indians who really own America." "It *is* the Indian who really owns America."

(5) A relative pronoun used as a subject takes a plural or singular verb to accord with its antecedent.

Boys who *throw* the discus . . . A *boy* who *throws* the discus.
Roy is among the *athletes* who *have competed* in the Olympics. [*Athletes* is the antecedent of *who.*]

Roy is the only *one* of our athletes who *has won* a gold medal. [*One*, not *athletes*, is the antecedent of *who*. The sentence means, "Of all our athletes Roy is the only *one* who *has won* a gold medal.]

(6) When used as subjects, *each*, *either*, *neither*, *another*, *anyone*, *anybody*, *anything*, *someone*, *somebody*, *something*, *one*, *everyone*, *everybody*, *everything*, *nobody*, *nothing* regularly take singular verbs.

Each *plans* to go to China.
Nobody *wants* to be left behind.
Someone *hopes* to go to Macao.

Everybody *is* excited.
Nobody *cares* to stay long.

None is plural or singular, depending on the other words in the sentence or in the immediately surrounding sentences (the context) which condition its meaning.

None *are* so sure of their knowledge as those who have only a little learning.
None *is* so sure of his knowledge as one who has only a little learning.

Any, all, more, most, and *some* are used with plural and singular verbs in much the same way as *none*.

(7) Collective nouns (and numbers denoting fixed quantity) usually take singular verbs because the group or quantity is usually regarded as a unit.

Our football team *has won* the championship. [The common use: *team* regarded as a unit]
Our football team *are quarreling* over their different positions. [Less common: individuals on the team regarded separately]

A thousand bushels *is* a good yield. [A unit]
A thousand bushels *were crated.* [Individual bushels]

The number of students *was* small. [*The number* is regularly taken as a unit.]
A number of students *were* sick. [*A number* refers to individuals.]

(8) A verb agrees with its subject, not with its predicate noun.

His favorite *meal is* hamburgers and potato chips.
Hamburgers and *potato chips are* his favorite meal.

Such sentences are often better recast so as to avoid the disagreement in number between subject and predicate noun.

His favorite meal consists of hamburgers and potato chips.

(9) Nouns plural in form but singular in meaning usually take singular verbs. In all doubtful cases a good dictionary should be consulted.

Regularly singular   aesthetics, civics, economics, genetics, linguistics, mathematics, measles, mumps, news, physics, semantics
Regularly plural   environs, trousers

Some nouns ending in *-ics* (such as *athletics, acoustics,* and *statistics*) are considered singular when they refer to an organized body of knowledge and plural when they refer to activities, qualities, or individual facts.

Athletics [activity in games] *is required* of every student.
Athletics [various games] *provide* good recreation.

Acoustics *is* an interesting study.
The acoustics of the hall *are* good.

Statistics *is* a science.
The statistics *were* easily *assembled.*

(10) A title of a single work or a word spoken of as a word, even when plural in form, takes a singular verb.

> *The Canterbury Tales is considered* rather plain-spoken even today.
> The London *Times is* a fine newspaper.

6b   Make a pronoun agree in number with its antecedent.

A singular antecedent (one which would take a singular verb) is referred to by a singular pronoun; a plural antecedent (one which would take a plural verb) is referred to by a plural pronoun.

(1) In formal English use a singular pronoun to refer to such antecedents as man, woman, person, one, anyone, anybody, someone, somebody, everyone, everybody, each, kind, sort, either, neither, no one, nobody. See also **6a(6).**

> A characteristic of modern *woman* is *her* (NOT *their*) desire to be equal in every way to men.

In informal English, plural pronouns are sometimes used after such antecedents when the sense is clearly plural.

> FORMAL   *Each* of the hockey players used *his* own style.
>
> INFORMAL   *Each* of the hockey players used *their* own style.

(2) Two or more antecedents joined by *and* are referred to by a plural pronoun; two or more singular antecedents joined by *or* or *nor* are referred to by a singular pronoun. If one or two antecedents joined by *or* is singular and one plural, the pronoun usually agrees with the nearer antecedent. See also **6a(2)** and **6a(3).**

> *Sally and Kim* have finished *their* practice teaching.
> Neither *Sally nor Kim* has finished *her* practice teaching.

(3) Collective nouns are referred to by singular or plural pronouns, depending on whether the collective noun is considered singular or plural. See also **6a(7).**

Special care should be taken to avoid making a collective noun *both* singular and plural within the same sentence.

> INCONSISTENT   The fraternity is planning their fall rush program. [*The fraternity* is first considered singular because of the choice of *is* and then plural because of *their.*]
>
> CONSISTENT   The *fraternity is planning its* fall rush program. [Singular] OR
>   The *fraternity are planning their* fall rush program. [Plural]

Agreement of subject and verb

NAME _____ SCORE _____

DIRECTIONS   In the following sentences underline each subject once and each verb twice. If all verbs in a sentence agree with their subjects, write *C* in the blank at the right; if not, circle the incorrect verb form and enter the correct form of the verb in the blank.

EXAMPLES

There (is) many scars upon our land.   *are*

One of the worst scars is caused by strip mining.   *C*

1. The trees and topsoil on many mountain ridges has been stripped away.   _____

2. The purpose of this despoiling of the mountains is to obtain minerals in a cheap way.   _____

3. The number of acres of ground ruined by strip mining are alarming.   _____

4. Almost four million acres of ground has been ruined in this way.   _____

5. There is many areas of strip mining in our country.   _____

6. One of the most depressing examples are seen in eastern Kentucky.   _____

7. Each of us know about the beauty of the mountains of Kentucky.   _____

8. But much of the beauty of this region has been destroyed by strip mining for coal.   _____

9. Many years ago the mineral rights to the land was sold by the people.   _____

10. The amount of money charged for these rights was unbelievably small, often no more than fifty cents an acre.   _____

11. At that time everyone were familiar with underground mines.   _____

12. But none of the people of eastern Kentucky were aware of strip mining. _____

13. Neither they nor their descendants was prepared for the results of their sale. _____

14. These results is all too obvious from the air. _____

15. The once beautiful ridges of forests now bears many unsightly wounds. _____

16. There are now acres of yellow soil showing among the trees. _____

17. Even worse, one frequently sees a ridge completely barren of trees except on its crown. _____

18. The ecologists knows about damage other than loss of beauty. _____

19. The sulfur in the exposed rocks oxidize. _____

20. The rains, of course, washes the sulfur into a mild solution of sulfuric acid. _____

21. Pools of this solution collects and eventually drains into the water table. _____

22. Soil, as well as streams, is affected. _____

23. Once-rich bottom land now support only marsh plants. _____

24. Fish and other aquatic life is killed. _____

25. David Nevin's essay "These Murdered Mountains" tell the story of the pathetic results of strip mining in eastern Kentucky. _____

NAME _____ SCORE _____

DIRECTIONS　In the following sentences underline each subject once and each verb twice. If all verbs in a sentence agree with their subjects, write *C* in the blank at the right; if not, circle the incorrect verb form and enter the correct form of the verb in the blank.

EXAMPLE

The <u>courts</u> in Kentucky (has) <u><u>supported</u></u> the strip miners' claims.　　　　　　　　　　　　　　　　　　　　　*have*

1. Kentucky, unlike other states, still recognizes the legal right of the strip mining companies to the mineral rights of the land despite the changes that have occurred.　　　　　　　　　　　　　　　　　　　　_____

2. Broad-form deeds, which was drawn up decades ago, say that the miners may do whatever is "necessary or convenient" to obtain the minerals from the land.　　　_____

3. None of the descendants of the original owners of the land have recourse under Kentucky laws.　　　　_____

4. Thus the mutilation of the mountains continue.　　　_____

5. Electric shovels, as tall as twenty-story buildings, moves as much as 350,000 pounds of dirt with a single bite.　_____

6. The number of acres that can be stripped in a single week is unbelievable.　　　　　　　　　　　　　　_____

7. A number of people, like former Secretary of the Interior Stewart Udall, opposes strip mining.　　　　_____

8. But the coal interests in Kentucky claims that strip mining is necessary to maintain our standard of living.　_____

9. The miners contend that the land they strip is worthless and that the tons of coal extracted is essential to the production of electrical power for the people of the area.　　　　　　　　　　　　　　　　　　　　_____

10. Neither the ecologist nor the farmer regard the land as worthless. _____

11. A million acres of land—or, for that matter, even a single acre—are a valuable commodity today when our world is running out of land. _____

12. One of the eloquent opponents of strip mining comment: "I believe that when man destroys his land, he begins to destroy himself." _____

13. Among the many possible solutions that has been presented is the process of reclaiming the land. _____

14. In a few places strip miners have reclaimed the land beautifully, but statistics shows that these areas are exceptions to the rule. _____

15. Kentucky, as well as eleven other states, have attempted to place some controls on strip mining. _____

16. In Kentucky the crests of ridges that have been strip mined are smoothed off and planted with grass and small trees. _____

17. But a mountain family living below a strip mine consider this procedure only a token effort on the part of the miners. _____

18. Elaborate procedures that restores the land to its original condition are used by strip miners in Europe. _____

19. But most people feel that economics prevents the use of such expensive processes in this country. _____

20. Again we find that there is no easy and cheap solution to an ecological problem. _____

Agreement of pronoun and antecedent

NAME _____ SCORE _____

DIRECTIONS   In each of the sentences below strike out the pronoun in parentheses that fails to agree with its antecedent. Then enter in the blank at the right the antecedent and the correct pronoun.

EXAMPLE

Each of us has (his, ~~their~~) own opinion about the greatest
source of pollution.   *Each - his*

1. When one considers ecology, too often (he considers, they consider) it someone else's problem.   _____

2. But everyone has contributed (his, their) part to the problem.   _____

3. A government agency may use (its, their) influence to counter pollution, but no agency can solve the problem alone.   _____

4. A person must take upon (himself, hisself, themselves) the responsibility for improving the air, the land, and the water.   _____

5. No one should feel (himself, hisself, themselves) free of blame for our ecological mess.   _____

6. A family that goes on a picnic and leaves (its, their) garbage scattered over the ground is to blame.   _____

7. A person who carelessly throws (his, their) cigarette or candy wrapper out the car window is to blame.   _____

8. A boater who tosses his beer can or soda bottle into the water assumes (his, their) share of the guilt.   _____

9. Of course, littering is only one way that man shows (his, their) disrespect for the environment.   _____

10. But the majority of people are unaware of the great amount of litter (it is, they are) responsible for.   _____

11. One of the senators who has raised (his, their) voice for ecology has proposed that Congress add this amendment to the Constitution: "Every person has the inalienable right to a decent environment. The United States and every state shall guarantee this right."   _____

12. Congress may vote (its, their) approval of the amendment and the various states may ratify it. _____

13. Nevertheless, the individual is still responsible for maintaining (his, their) right to a decent environment. _____

14. Craig and John, two students at the University of Houston, spent (his, their) summer working with a local ecological group. _____

15. Neither Craig nor John knew when (he, they) became affiliated with the group that ecology could require so much time. _____

16. Each worked in the area (he, they) felt the most concern for. _____

17. The group included about twenty other students who devoted (theirselves, themselves) to studying the various ecological problems of the area. _____

18. A study group did not always agree about what (it, they) thought should be done about a problem. _____

19. But none of the members of the group felt (his, their) time wasted in learning the facts they would need to make wise decisions. _____

20. And all decided (he, they) would become permanently involved in an active ecological group. _____

7

Use the appropriate form of the verb.

The verb is our most inflected part of speech. It changes form to show both tense and number: he *eats*, they *eat*, he or they *ate*. Most verbs have four distinct forms or inflections (*write, writes, writing, written*), but a few have only three (*set, sets, setting*), and some have five or more. The verb *be*, our most irregular verb, has eight inflections: *be, am, is, are, being, was, were, been*.

Many of the errors in verb usage come from failure to distinguish between the present tense, or time, and the past tense. These two forms of the verb, along with the past participle, make up the three "principal parts." If we know the principal parts of a verb—the regular present form (*write*), the simple past (*wrote*), and the past participle (*written*)—we can, with a little thought, use the verb correctly in all six tenses. Note how the six tenses are built on the principal parts of the "irregular" verb *write* and the "regular" verb *use*.

Principal parts

PRESENT	write	use
PAST	wrote	used
PAST PARTICIPLE	written	used

Tenses

PRESENT	I write	I use
FUTURE	I will write	I will use [Built on the present]
PAST	I wrote	I used
PRESENT PERFECT	I have written	I have used ⎱ [Built on
PAST PERFECT	I had written	I had used ⎬ the past
FUTURE PERFECT	I shall have written	I shall have used ⎰ participle]

7a   Use the appropriate tense form.

The dictionary lists all verbs under the present form—the first of the three principal parts. For all irregular verbs (such as *write, run, see*) the dictionary gives the past tense (*wrote, ran, saw*), the past participle (*written, run, seen*), and the present participle (*writing, running, seeing*). In the case of regular verbs (such as *use*) the past tense and the past participle, when not given, are understood to be formed in the regular way by adding *d* or *ed*.

> NONSTANDARD   Mike sung in the glee club. [Past tense desired; dictionary gives *sang* as the correct form for the past tense.]
>
> STANDARD   Mike *sang* in the glee club.

Do not confuse verbs similar in meaning and spelling, such as *lay* and *lie,* *set* and *sit, raise* and *rise.* The verb *lay* (past, *laid;* past participle, *laid*), meaning to place something, always takes an object.

> The scientist *lays* (OR *is laying*) the moon rocks in the drawer.   [Present]
> Yesterday he *laid* the rocks on the table.   [Past]
> Every day he *has laid* them in a different place.   [Past participle]

The verb *lie* (*lay, lain*), meaning to recline, never takes an object.

> I *lie* (OR *am lying*) in my bunk.   [Present]
> Last week I *lay* in my bunk.   [Past]
> I *have lain* in my bunk daily.   [Past participle]

The verb *set* (*set, set*), meaning to place something, always takes an object.

> Charlie *sets* (OR *is setting*) his muddy boots on the dresser, where he *set* them yesterday, and where he *has* always *set* them.

The verb *sit* (*sat, sat*), meaning to rest on a seat, never takes an object.

> He now *sits* (OR *is sitting*) cross-legged on the floor, where he *sat* yesterday, and where he *has sat* every day.

The verb *raise* (*raised, raised*), meaning to lift something, always takes an object.

> He now *raises* (OR *is raising*) the heaviest barbell. He *raised* it yesterday, and he *has* often *raised* it.

The verb *rise* (*rose, risen*), meaning to get up, never takes an object.

> I *rise* (OR *am rising*) reluctantly this morning. I *rose* reluctantly yesterday, and I often *have risen* reluctantly.

Note: In the passive voice the word that is the object in the active voice becomes the subject: "The moon rocks were laid in the cabinet." Verbs that take no object—such as *lie, sit, rise*—cannot be used in the passive voice.

7b   Use logical tense forms in sequence, focusing on the tense of the main or governing verb.

Make a subordinate verb, an infinitive, or a participle conform logically in time with the main verb.

> He *slept* after he *had finished* (NOT *finished*) cutting the grass.
> He *was sleeping* where the grass *had been* (NOT *was*) cut.
> He hoped *to regain* (NOT *to have regained*) his energy.
> *Having slept* (NOT *sleeping*) for an hour, he *was* still *exhausted.*

Caution: Avoid needless shifts in tense.

> SHIFT   The young artist completed the painting and immediately sells it. [Needless shift from past tense to present tense]
>
> IMPROVED   The young artist *completed* the painting and immediately *sold* it.

Difficulties with verbs

NAME _____ SCORE _____

DIRECTIONS In the following sentences enter the correct form of the verb in the blank within the sentence and also in the numbered space at the right. After your answers have been checked, read the sentences aloud several times to accustom your ear to the correct verb.

TAKES AN OBJECT   TAKES NO OBJECT
set, set, set   *sit, sat, sat*

Often when one (1) _____ down to consider   1. _____

ecology, he thinks about it as a subject in textbooks that

(2) _____ down accounts of other people's   2. _____

troubles. Recently I drove down to my beach house and

found that ecology was my problem too, because less

than five hundred feet from my house (3) _____   3. _____

an oil derrick. The oil rig was (4) _____ in clear   4. _____

view of my house. The oil company had (5) _____   5. _____

it up so that no matter where I (6) _____ in my   6. _____

living room I was looking at the derrick.

TAKES AN OBJECT   TAKES NO OBJECT
raise, raised, raised   *rise, rose, risen*

The oil company had (7) _____ the derrick in one   7. _____

weekend. And it now (8) _____ over one hundred   8. _____

feet in the air. At night I could see it (9) _____   9. _____

into the air, its lights outlining its defiant shape. Several

times I (10) _____ to look out at it because the   10. _____

pumping machinery ground away so noisily that I could

not sleep. Then when the sun had (11) _____   11. _____

the next morning, there the derrick stood, its ugly shape

blocking my view of the ocean. As I (12) _____   12. _____

the flag on the porch, I could see the men at the derrick

scurrying here and there.

TAKES AN OBJECT
lay, laid, laid

TAKES NO OBJECT
lie, lay, lain

After breakfast I went down to (13) _____ on the beach and to collect the various shells and sand dollars that are always (14) _____ around after the tide has gone out. As I (15) _____ my towel down I noticed that something unusual (16) _____ on the white sand. (17) _____ on top of the sand and pebbles were areas of black sludge. I found that the spot where I had (18) _____ my towel was coated with oil. And if I had (19) _____ down, my new white bathing suit would have been badly stained. For today I had to (20) _____ aside my plans for the beach.

13. _____

14. _____

15. _____

16. _____

17. _____

18. _____

19. _____

20. _____

Difficulties with verbs

NAME _____ SCORE _____

DIRECTIONS In the following sentences enter the correct form of the verb in the blank within the sentence and also in the numbered space at the right. After your answers have been checked, read the sentences aloud several times to accustom your ear to the correct verb.

see, saw, seen

What I (1) _____ at the beach angered me, but what I had not (2) _____ would have ter-rified me.

1. _____

2. _____

ride, rode, ridden

After I had (3) _____ home, I began to in-vestigate offshore and shoreline drilling. I (4) _____ over to the public library to do my research.

3. _____

4. _____

write, wrote, written

I found several encyclopedia articles (5) _____ on the subject. Then I investigated the ecology books that had been (6) _____ in the past three years. The people who (7) _____ the material dis-agreed about the advisability of offshore and shoreline drilling, but all of them discussed one effect of the drill-ing that I had not thought about.

5. _____

6. _____

7. _____

take, took, taken

It has (8) _____ several centuries for the earth to produce the oil we are now pumping out of the ground, but it will (9) _____ only a few years for us to deplete our oil supply if we continue our present rate of drilling. In other words, what it (10) _____ the earth several generations to produce, we can use up in a single generation.

8. _____

9. _____

10. _____

I also (11) _____ to understand what happens
when underground mineral deposits are removed. The
land (12) _____ to sink. The sinking process
had already (13) _____ at my beach, although
I could not yet see the effect.

11. _____

12. _____

13. _____

use, used, used

Our shorelines (14) _____ to recede very slowly,
but modern civilization has speeded up the process so
that now we are (15) _____ to seeing water
claim our land in a few years' time. In ten or fifteen
years water would inundate the area around my beach
house.

14. _____

15. _____

give, gave, given

Until the oil derrick appeared in front of my beach
house, I had never (16) _____ ecology much
attention. Now I was concerned because I was personally
affected. But what I learned next (17) _____
me something else to consider.

16. _____

17. _____

choose, chose, chosen

The company that had (18) _____ to build
the derrick was one that I worked for every summer during college and the company that I would probably
(19) _____ to affiliate myself with after college.
In addition, I (20) _____ to drive a car every
day that needed the gas and oil the company supplied.

18. _____

19. _____

20. _____

Difficulties with verbs

NAME _____ SCORE _____

DIRECTIONS   In the following sentences strike out every verb form that is incorrectly used and write the correct form in the blank at the right. Enter C in the blank after each sentence that contains no verb form incorrectly used.

EXAMPLE

E. D. Fales, Jr., a reporter, has ~~wrote~~ an account of what he saw when he took a survey of our country's mountains.   *written*

1. Fales wanted to see as many mountain ranges as possible; thus he takes advantage of all types of conveyances—plane, automobile, aerial cable car, and canoe.   _____

2. When he finished the tour, he ask himself and us the question, "Can our mountains be saved?"   _____

3. For centuries man has been drew to the mountains for inspiration, and he has set down many words in praise of them.   _____

4. When men have drank in the beauty of the mountains' wild terrain, they have composed poems and painted pictures.   _____

5. Because man loves the mountains, he chooses to be as close to them as possible.   _____

6. A few decades ago man begun to develop the mountain areas, and his desire to civilize the wild places has grown stronger each year.   _____

7. Areas that once were hid from view now have superhighways running through them.   _____

8. Cades Cove, a farm community in the Smoky Mountains that once laid far from modern man's world, is now accessible by roads, and hundreds of tourists drive through it every day.   _____

9. Few mountain peaks lie beyond the reach of real estate developers, mining projects, and recreation planners.   _____

10. Fales claims he counted six mountain peaks that have became displays for high school and college initials.   _____

11. Many mountain peaks were use to develop badly planned ski resorts that destroyed the beauty of the setting. _____

12. From the air most of our mountains look as though gigantic plows had been dragged across them. _____

13. Fales was heartbroke by the sights he saw and by man's continued rush to develop all our wild places. _____

14. In New Hampshire developers have ran a new superhighway through the White Mountains and now want to extend it straight under the Great Stone Face, which Nathaniel Hawthorne wrote his famous sketch about. _____

15. Having stood for centuries untouched, Idaho's majestic Sawtooth–White Clouds Mountains are now threatened by a gigantic open-pit mine. _____

16. In Maine Fales found a mountain peak that four developers were trying to have turned into a recreational development. _____

17. Fales feels that Americans are becoming concerned about their mountain peaks, as is demonstrated by the reaction of the citizens of Boulder, Colorado, to the increasing development of the Rocky Mountain slopes that lie around the city. _____

18. The citizens of Boulder have spoke out against the development of the mountains for several years, and now they are taxing themselves to buy up mountain land. _____

19. Having wanted to keep the mountain areas around their city unspoiled, the citizens spend $500,000 a year to buy up the land. _____

20. People have finally came to realize that the mountains belong to all the people and that their beauty should not be sacrificed for any amount of money. _____

MECHANICS

Capitals / Italics   cap 9 / ital 10

9 Capitalize words in accordance with general usage.

9a First words Use capitals to mark the beginning of (1) each sentence, even if it is directly quoted within another sentence; (2) each line of poetry; and (3) the title of a book, even if the first word is *a* or *the*.

My friend asked, "Have you read *The Last of the Mohicans?*"

9b Proper names Capitalize words referring to specific persons, places, organizations, races, or things (*Shakespeare, America*); adjectives derived from proper names (*Shakespearean, American*); titles of respect preceding the name of a person (*Captain* Smith, *Senator* Jones); words denoting family relationship when used as titles or alone in place of the name, but not when preceded by a possessive (*Brother* James; a trip with *Father;* a trip with my *father*); and other words used as an essential part of a proper name (Mills *College,* Webster *High School*). But articles, prepositions, and conjunctions used as a part of a proper name are usually not capitalized, except as the first word of the title of a book. The pronoun *I* and the interjection *O* are always capitalized, as are most nouns referring to the Deity (the *Saviour,* the *Almighty*).

Caution: Avoid needless capitals. Note especially that the seasons (*spring, summer, fall, autumn, winter*) are capitalized only when personified, as in poetry; that *north, south, east,* and *west* are capitalized only in referring to a specific region (the history of the *West*); that the names of studies are capitalized only when specific (*history, History 2*) or when derived from a proper name (*Spanish*).

9c Abbreviations Abbreviations are usually capitalized or not capitalized according to the capitalization of the word abbreviated: *m.p.h. (miles per hour*); *H.R. (House of Representatives); naut. (nautical); Pac. (Pacific*).

10 Italicize (underline) words in accordance with general usage.

Use italics to indicate titles of books, long plays, or magazines; names of ships and aircraft; foreign words; and letters, figures, or words spoken of as such.

He read *Treasure Island* while taking a cruise on the *Majestic.*
He soon became *persona non grata.*
Drop the 3 from 8763; then omit *c* to make *fact* read *fat.*

Caution: Use italics sparingly as a means of giving emphasis to a word or a group of words.

11

In ordinary writing avoid most abbreviations, and write out numbers whenever they can be expressed in one or two words.

11a   Spell out all titles except *Mr., Messrs., Mrs., Mmes., Dr.,* and *St.* (for *Saint*, NOT for *Street*). These are usually spelled out when not followed by a proper name.

11b   Spell out names of states (*Texas*, NOT *Tex.*), countries (*United States*, NOT *U.S.*), months (*August*, NOT *Aug.*), days of the week (*Monday*, NOT *Mon.*), and units of measurement (*pounds*, NOT *lbs.*).

11c   Spell out *Street* (*Lee Street*, NOT *Lee St.*), *Road, Park, Company*, and similar words used as part of a proper name.

11d   Spell out the words *volume, chapter*, and *page* and the names of courses of study.

> The notes on *chemistry* (NOT *chem.*) are taken from *chapter* 9, *page* 46 (NOT *ch. 9, p. 46*, except in footnotes).

11e   Spell out first names (*Charles*, NOT *Chas.*, White).

Permissible Abbreviations: In addition to the abbreviations mentioned in **11a**, the following are permissible and usually desirable: *Jr., Sr., Esq.*, and degrees such as *D.D., LL.D., M.D.*, after proper nouns; A.D., B.C., A.M., P.M., *No.* or *no.*, and $, with dates or numerals; *ECA, GOP, RFC, TVA, WAC*, and so on, for names of certain agencies or organizations. The following Latin abbreviations are in general use, but the English terms are often spelled out in formal writing, as indicated in parentheses: *i.e. (that is), e.g. (for example), viz. (namely), cf. (compare), etc. (and so forth), vs. (versus).* Use *etc.* sparingly. Never write *and etc.; etc.* comes from *et cetera*, of which *et* means *and*.

11f   In general spell out numbers that require only one or two words, but use figures for other numbers.

> *twenty* years, *fifty thousand* dollars, *165* years from now, a sum of $2.27, *12.5 million* people, exactly *4,568,305* votes

Special Usage Regarding Numbers: Use figures for dates (*1956*; May *1, 1957*); for addresses (*65* Broadway); for identification numbers (Channel *4*, Route *22*); for pages of a book (page *40*); for decimals and percentages (*.57* inches, *10* percent); and for the hour of the day with A.M. or P.M. (*4:00* P.M.). Normally use figures for a series of numbers (a room *25* feet long, *18* feet wide, and *10* feet high). Spell out any numeral at the beginning of a sentence.

Capitals, italics, abbreviations, and numbers

NAME _____ SCORE _____

DIRECTIONS   In the following sentences (1) capitalize where necessary, (2) cross through needless capitals, (3) underline all words that should be italicized, and (4) correct poor usage of abbreviations and numbers. Enter all corrections in the blanks at the right. Write *C* after each line that needs no revision.

EXAMPLE

All Ȼollege students should read the book Silent Spring.   *college, Silent Spring*

1. Students everywhere—in the north, south, east, and   _____
   west—have become concerned about the Earth and   _____
   what americans are doing to it.   _____

2. Courses in Sociology and Science emphasize ecol-   _____
   ogy; special lectures in ecology are common oc-   _____
   currences in Junior Colleges and Universities.   _____

3. At galveston college in Galveston, Tex., students   _____
   in biology 101 organized a series of lectures that   _____
   featured speakers from organizations like Friends   _____
   Of The Earth and Zero Population Growth.   _____

4. The lecture topics included "Local Pollution Prob-   _____
   lems," "the Killing of the Gulf of Mexico," and   _____
   "Important Studies In Ecology Since Rachel Car-   _____
   son's Silent Spring."   _____

5. Over 200 students, or 75% of the college's enroll-   _____
   ment, attended the 1-hr. lectures by scientists,   _____
   Medical Doctors, college professors, and etc.   _____

6. The lectures also attracted High School Seniors,   _____
   PTA groups, and city officials like the Mayor and   _____
   the City Council.   _____

7. As a result of the program, students and adults   _____
   began reading books like Science and Survival,   _____
   joining groups like the Sierra club, and cleaning   _____
   up the 75 mis. of beaches that line the Gulf in the   _____
   galveston area.   _____

Capitals, italics, abbreviations, and numbers

NAME _____ SCORE _____

DIRECTIONS   Follow the directions for Exercise 11-1.

1. Barry Commoner, of Washington Univ. in Saint   _____
   Louis, hopes that ecology is not a passing fad.   _____
2. Some optimistic ecologists, like Commoner, say,   _____
   "we are in a period of grace"; they believe we   _____
   have about 30 yrs. to save our environment.   _____
3. Other ecologists sound like jeremiahs; "the end of _____
   the World," they claim, "Is clearly in sight regard- _____
   less of what Mankind does."   _____
4. Certainly there are some bad signs: Apollo Ten   _____
   Astronauts reported seeing smog above Los Angeles   _____
   from twenty-five thousand miles away; airline pilots _____
   can see smoke as far as 70 miles from even the   _____
   cities we consider clean, like Missoula, Mon.; lake _____
   Michigan is presently doomed to die in 20 yrs.   _____
5. Countries other than the U.S. have reason for con- _____
   cern, too: the Rhine river is known as europe's   _____
   sewer; residents in tokyo must sometimes wear gas   _____
   masks; black snow once fell in smakland, a swed-   _____
   ish province; the once crystal-clear lake Geneva   _____
   now supports few Trout or Perch.   _____
6. Pollution is serious enough for the president of   _____
   the United States to call it "The great question of _____
   the 70's" in his state of the union message.   _____
7. Ecology is derived from a greek word, oikos,   _____
   which means "house"; and it is clear that man   _____
   must take better care of his house if he is to con- _____
   tinue his Existence.   _____
8. Hopefully, the latter half of the Twentieth Century _____
   will be the time when man shows real concern for   _____
   his house—"the good earth."   _____

The Comma   ,/ 12

12

Use the comma in order to make clear the meaning of the sentence.

The reading of sentences aloud to determine where pauses and changes in voice pitch naturally come will often show where commas should be placed. But sentence structure is usually a more reliable test.

The many different uses of the comma may be grouped under a very few principles and mastered with comparative ease by anyone who understands the structure of the sentence. These principles, which cover the normal practice of the best contemporary writers, are adequate for the needs of the average college student. He may note that skilled writers sometimes employ the comma in unusual ways to express delicate shades of meaning. Such variations can safely be made only by the writer who has first learned to apply the following major principles:

Use the comma—

a to separate main clauses joined by *and, but, or, nor,* or *for;*
b to set off certain introductory elements;
c to separate items in a series, including coordinate adjectives modifying the same noun;
d to set off parenthetical elements (especially nonrestrictive clauses, phrases, and words).

12a   Commas are used between main clauses joined by the coordinating conjunctions *and, but, or, nor, for.*[1]

$$
\text{PATTERN} \quad \text{MAIN CLAUSE,} \left\{ \begin{array}{l} and \\ but \\ or \\ nor \\ for \end{array} \right\} \text{MAIN CLAUSE.}
$$

A picture by Titian sold for almost four million dollars in London, and the man who bought it felt he got a bargain.

The buyer refused to comment on whether the picture would go to America, but art critics believe it inevitably will.

The British National Gallery could not bid high enough, nor was it possible to raise the money from private sources in England.

---

[1] *Yet* is occasionally used as a coordinating conjunction equivalent to *but*. Informal writing frequently uses *so* as a coordinating conjunction, but careful writers usually avoid the *so* sentence by subordinating one of the clauses: see **24b**.

It is hoped that there will be more money available in the future, for it is sad to see Britain lose her long-held art treasures.

Caution: Do not confuse a simple sentence containing a compound predicate (no comma needed) with a compound sentence (comma needed).

Mary iced the birthday cake and served it to her guests.   [No pause and therefore no comma needed between the parts of the compound predicate]

Even more objectionable than a comma between parts of a compound predicate is the use of a comma before a conjunction which joins merely two words (*boy* and *girl, pure* and *simple*) or two phrases (*to work* and *to play*) or two subordinate clauses (*that he ran for office* and *that he won*).

At times, the comma is used to set off what seems to be merely the second part of a compound predicate, or even a phrase. Closer examination, however, usually discloses that the material following the comma is actually a main clause with some words "understood"; the use of the comma emphasizes the distinction between the principal ideas in the sentence. Note the following sentences, in which the implied matter is inserted in brackets:

Growing up is largely learning to settle for what is possible, and for the young [growing up] is not always a happy process.   —LONDON TIMES
The clothes of teenagers have changed amazingly in the past ten years, and their ideas [have changed] even more so.

Exceptions to 12a: The comma before the coordinating conjunctions *and* and *or* (and sometimes *but* or *for*) may be omitted if the main clauses are short.

The dog barked and the burglar ran.

A semicolon is often preferable to a comma when the main clauses are very long. The use of the semicolon is strongly desirable, if not absolutely necessary, when one clause contains commas; the semicolon enables the reader to see at a glance the chief break in the sentence. See also **14a.**

The people shall not be deprived or abridged of their right to speak, to write, or to publish their sentiments; and the freedom of the press as one of the great hallmarks of liberty shall be inviolable.   —BILL OF RIGHTS

12b   Commas follow such introductory elements as adverb clauses, long phrases, mild interjections, or transitional expressions. (Note that in speaking a pause normally marks such commas.)

PATTERNS   ADVERB CLAUSE, MAIN CLAUSE.
LONG PHRASE, MAIN CLAUSE.
INTERJECTION, MAIN CLAUSE.
TRANSITIONAL EXPRESSION, MAIN CLAUSE.

(1) When an adverb clause precedes the main clause, it is usually followed by a comma.

Although our family had enjoyed the vacation, we were ready to go home. [Read the sentence aloud, and notice the pause after the adverb clause.]

Many writers omit the comma after short introductory clauses, and sometimes after longer ones, when the omission does not make for difficult reading. In the following sentences, the commas may be used or omitted at the option of the writer:

> After it rained (,) the sun shone.
> When he drove (,) he was conscious of the traffic laws.   [When the subject of the introductory clause is repeated in the main clause, the comma is usually unnecessary.]

Note: When the adverb clause *follows* the main clause, there is usually no pause and no need for a comma.

> PATTERN   MAIN CLAUSE   ADVERB CLAUSE.
> They were seated before the other couple came.
> We talked until the stars came out.

Such adverb clauses, however, are set off by commas if they are parenthetical or loosely connected with the rest of the sentence—especially if the subordinating conjunction seems equivalent to a coordinating conjunction (or if a distinct pause is required in the reading).

> The new Wimbledon tennis champion won easily, although she was only nineteen.   [*Although* is equivalent to *but*.]
> She seemed serene and relaxed, whether she was behind in the match or ahead.

(2) A long phrase preceding a main clause usually requires a comma.

> Inhaling deeply and stretching himself to keep every muscle alert, the champion began the match.   —LONDON TIMES

Introductory phrases containing a gerund, a participle, or an infinitive, even though short, must often be followed by a comma to prevent misreading.

> Because of their decision to strike, the miners walked out.
> After eating, the cat washed her face.

Short introductory prepositional phrases, except when they are transitional expressions, are seldom followed by commas.

> After yesterday's race the horse was lame.
> In case of injury I have insurance.

(3) Use a comma after a mild interjection at the beginning of a sentence.

> Oh, I wish he were here.
> Whew, that was close.

(4) Use a comma after a transitional expression.

> In short, I do not wish to go.
> On the other hand, the trip would be pleasant.

12c   Commas are used between items in a series, including coordinate adjectives modifying the same noun.

73

(1) Items in a series

PATTERNS   ITEM 1, ITEM 2, ITEM 3.
              ITEM 1, ITEM 2, *and* ITEM 3.

The water was *clear, blue, quiet.*   [Words in a series, form *a, b, c*]
The water was *clear, blue,* and *quiet.*   [Form *a, b,* and *c*]
The water was *clear* and *blue* and *quiet.*   [Form *a* and *b* and *c.* Commas are omitted when *and* is used throughout the series.]

The men walked *in the rain, in the hail,* and *in the snow.*   [Phrases in a series]
That we were tired, that we were hungry, and *that we were lost* was quite evident.   [Subordinate clauses in a series]
He arrived, he saw the employer's daughter, and *he took the job.*   [Main clauses in a series]

The final comma is often omitted, especially by newspapers, when the series takes the form *a, b,* and *c.* But students are usually advised to use the comma throughout the series, if only because the comma is sometimes needed to prevent confusion.

CONFUSING   Mother baked custard, cherry, raisin and apple pies.   [Was the last pie a mixture of raisins and apples?]
CLEAR   Mother baked custard, cherry, raisin, and apple pies. OR
           Mother baked custard, cherry, and raisin and apple pies.

(2) Coordinate adjectives

Adjectives are coordinate and take a comma between them when they modify the same word or word group. Notice in the following examples that the natural pauses between coordinate adjectives are indicated by commas.

a tall, white building   [*Tall* and *white* are coordinate adjectives modifying the word *building.*]
a tall, white post office building   [*Tall* and *white* modify *post office building,* which is pronounced as a unit.]

Tests for Coordinate Adjectives

Coordinate adjectives ordinarily have a reversible word order; adjectives which are not coordinate do not.

COORDINATE   healthy, happy children   [Logical: happy, healthy children]
NOT COORDINATE   six healthy children   [Illogical: healthy six children]

Coordinate adjectives may have *and* inserted between them without changing the meaning.

COORDINATE   tall, handsome boys   [Logical: tall and handsome boys]
NOT COORDINATE   six tall boys   [Illogical: six and tall boys]

12d   Commas are used to set off parenthetical elements ("interrupters") such as nonrestrictive words, clauses, and phrases. Restrictive words, clauses, and phrases are not set off.

74

(1) **Use a comma after a parenthetical element at the beginning of a sentence, before a parenthetical element at the end, and both before and after one within a sentence.**

> *My friends,* we must guard our liberty.
> We must guard our liberty, *my friends.*
> We must, *my friends,* guard our liberty.

> *He repeated,* "Liberty is precious."
> "Liberty is precious," *he repeated.*
> "Liberty," *he repeated,* "is precious."

Caution: When two commas are needed to set off a parenthetical element within the sentence, do not forget the second comma. To use one comma but not the second makes reading more difficult than the omission of both commas does.

CONFUSING	The book, of course will be completed.
CLEAR	The book, of course, will be completed. OR The book of course will be completed.
CONFUSING	The book, we have been assured is ready for publication.
CLEAR	The book, we have been assured, is ready for publication.

(2) **Nonrestrictive clauses and phrases are set off by commas. Restrictive clauses and phrases are not set off.**

Adjective clauses and phrases are nonrestrictive when they merely add information about a word already identified. Such modifiers are parenthetical and may be omitted. Since they are not essential to the meaning of the main clause, they are set off by commas.

> William Penn, *who was the leader of the Quakers,* was granted land by Charles II.   ["William Penn was granted land by Charles II" is true without the nonessential *who was the leader of the Quakers.*]
> Philadelphia, *which Penn founded,* is now a fine city.
> Philadelphia, *founded by Penn,* is now a fine city.

Adjective clauses and phrases are restrictive when they are needed to identify the word they modify. Such clauses and phrases limit or restrict the meaning of the sentence and cannot be omitted; therefore no commas should be used.

> The man *who led the Quakers* obtained land from Charles II.   ["The man obtained land from Charles II" is true only with the essential *who led the Quakers.*]
> The city *founded by the Quakers* was Philadelphia.

Adjective clauses beginning with *that* are restrictive. Adjective clauses beginning with *who (whom, whose)* and *which* may be restrictive or nonrestrictive.

Your voice can help you distinguish between restrictive and nonrestrictive modifiers. As you read the following sentences aloud, note that you neither pause nor lower the pitch of your voice for the restrictive passages. On the other hand, you normally "set off" the nonrestrictive modifiers by using definite pauses and by changing the pitch of your voice.

RESTRICTIVE   The person *holding the winning ticket* should come forward.
NONRESTRICTIVE   Helen, *holding the winning ticket,* received the prize.

RESTRICTIVE   A man *who works in a bank* must understand and enjoy figures.
NONRESTRICTIVE   My father, *who works in a bank,* enjoys working with figures.

Carefully study the meaning of the sentences below. Also read each one aloud, and let your voice help you to distinguish between restrictive and non-restrictive clauses and phrases.

NONRESTRICTIVE

Cairo, *which is on the River Nile,* is a very old city.   [The *which* clause, adding information about a city already identified, is parenthetical and not essential to the main clause, *Cairo is a very old city.* Commas needed.]
Cairo, *situated on the River Nile,* is a very old city.   [Phrase]

RESTRICTIVE

A city *that is old* is often in need of modern improvements.   [The clause *that is old* is essential to the main clause. No commas.]
A city *in need of modern improvements* has hard work ahead.   [Phrase]

NONRESTRICTIVE

My brother, *who is paying his own way through school,* must work every summer.   [The italicized clause adds information about a person already identified. Commas mark pauses and change in voice pitch.]
My brother, *paying his own way through school,* works hard every summer. [Phrase]

RESTRICTIVE

Any boy *who wants to pay his own way through school* must work hard.   [The *who* clause is essential to the identification of *any boy.*]
Any boy *paying his own way through school* must work hard.   [Phrase]

Sometimes a clause or phrase may be either restrictive or nonrestrictive; the writer signifies his meaning by the proper use of the comma.

NONRESTRICTIVE   He liked his teachers, *who also liked him.* [He liked all his teachers. In turn, all of them liked him.]

RESTRICTIVE   He liked his teachers *who also liked him.* [He liked only those teachers who also liked him.]

(3) Nonrestrictive appositives, contrasted elements, geographical names, and items in dates and addresses are set off by commas.

APPOSITIVES AND CONTRASTED ELEMENTS

Appositives are usually nonrestrictive (parenthetical), merely adding information about a person or thing already identified. Such appositives are set off by commas, which mark distinct pauses and changes in voice pitch. Note that

76

most appositives may be readily expanded into nonrestrictive clauses. In other words, the principle underlying the use of commas to set off nonrestrictive clauses also applies here.

> Lynn, *my nephew*, is now in India.   [The appositive *my nephew* is equivalent to the nonrestrictive clause *who is my nephew*. Note the distinct pauses and changes in voice pitch.]
>
> Ulysses S. Grant, *the victorious general in the Civil War*, was later a mediocre president.   [The appositive is equivalent to the nonrestrictive clause *who was the victorious general in the Civil War*.]
>
> My companions were James White, *Esq.*, William Smith, *M.D.*, and Rufus L. Block, *Ph.D.*   [Abbreviated titles after names are treated as appositives.]
>
> Our dreams, *not our failures*, should direct our future lives.   [The contrasted element is a sort of negative appositive.]
>
> My cousin, *not my nephew*, has the key.
>
> High grades come from hard work, *not from idleness*.

At times appositives are restrictive, and commas are omitted.

> My nephew *Lynn* is the one who is in India.   [*Lynn*, not some other nephew, is in India.]
>
> The victor *Grant* was not as outstanding as a president as he had been as a general.   [*Grant* restricts the meaning, telling what victor was not as outstanding a president as he had been a general.]
>
> George *the Third* was King of England in 1771.   [An appositive that is part of a title is restrictive.]
>
> The word *decibels* has come into increasing use in recent years.
>
> Both Francis Bacon *the philosopher* and Francis Bacon *the painter* have contributed to man's understanding of his world.

GEOGRAPHICAL NAMES, ITEMS IN DATES AND ADDRESSES

> Knoxville, Tennessee, lies at the foot of the Smoky Mountains.   [*Tennessee* may be thought of as equivalent to the nonrestrictive clause *which is in Tennessee*.]
>
> Send the letter to Mr. J. L. Karnes, Clayton, Delaware 19938.   [The zip code is not separated by a comma from the name of the state.]
>
> Wednesday, July 20, 1971, in Rome   [Students are usually advised not to drop the comma after the year, as in "July 20, 1971 in Rome."]
>
> October, 1822, in Boston   OR   October 1822 in Boston   [Commas are often omitted when the day of the month is not given.]

(4) Parenthetical words, phrases, or clauses (inserted expressions), words in direct address, and absolute elements are set off by commas.

PARENTHETICAL EXPRESSIONS

Actually, the term "parenthetical" is correctly applied to all nonrestrictive elements discussed under **12d**; but the term is more commonly applied to such expressions as *on the other hand, in the first place, in fact, to tell the truth, however, that is, for example, I hope, I report, he says.* The term would apply equally well to expressions inserted in dialogue: *he said, he observed, he* *protested,* and so on. Parenthetical expressions that come at the beginning of a sentence are treated in both **12b** and **12d**.

Students without funds, *for example,* may now borrow money easily.
The judge held, *in fact,* that the firm was liable.
We must, *on the other hand,* consider our budget.
"The next meeting," *she announced,* "will be today."
The rest of the activities, *however,* were cancelled. [When *however* means "nevertheless," it is usually set off by commas.]
Use seat belts *however* well you drive. [When *however* means "no matter how," it is not parenthetical and therefore is not set off by commas.]

Parenthetical expressions causing little if any pause in reading are frequently not set off by commas: *also, too, indeed, perhaps, at least, likewise,* and so forth. The writer must use his own judgment.

Sewing is *indeed* a useful hobby.
The boat *perhaps* will be repaired by Saturday.
Government aid is *of course* needed. OR Government aid is, *of course,* needed.

DIRECT ADDRESS

Here, *Susan,* is your mistake.
This, *fellow members,* will be our club project.
I appeal, *sir,* to your sense of fair play.

ABSOLUTE ELEMENTS

Expressions independent of the rest of the sentence are called absolute elements.

Rain or shine, the mail must go through. [Absolute phrase]
He had no intention of stopping, *his mind being made up.* [Nominative absolute]
Well, we will hope for the best. [Mild interjection]
There is no mail, *is there?* [Echo question]

12e Occasionally a comma, though not called for by any of the major principles already discussed, may be needed to prevent misreading.

Use **12e** sparingly to justify your commas. In a general sense, nearly all commas are used to prevent misreading or to make reading easier. But your mastery of the comma will come largely through application of the more specific major principles (*a, b, c, d*) to the structure of the sentence.

CONFUSING Outside the trees were weighted with snow. [*Outside* may be at first mistaken for a preposition.]
CLEAR Outside, the trees were weighted with snow. [*Outside* is clearly an adverb.]

CONFUSING Above all the guests must be made to feel welcome.
CLEAR Above all, the guests must be made to feel welcome.

Commas between main clauses

NAME _____ SCORE _____

DIRECTIONS   In the following sentences, insert an inverted caret (V) between main clauses and add a comma or semicolon as needed; in the blank at the right enter the comma or the semicolon plus the coordinating conjunction. If the sentence is correct, write *C* in the blank at the right. (Note that some of the sentences are not compound. Bracket any subordinate clauses that appear incidentally.)

EXAMPLE

Through our mistakes we are gradually learning to be more considerate of our environment,ᵛand hopefully this new concern does not come too late. ___, *and*___

1. Ecology is a new science, only seventy years old and general public interest in it is newer still, less than ten years. _____

2. Many things that we do to improve our environment seem practical at the time but they sometimes produce disastrous results that we do not anticipate. _____

3. For example, DDT seemed to be man's salvation from mosquitoes that carry malaria, from the boll weevil that affects cotton, and from a variety of other insects that plague the farmers' crops but this seeming cure-all also did enough damage to man and his environment for it to be labeled a curse by many scientists. _____

4. What man did not anticipate about DDT was that it would contaminate almost everything in the environment and that this contamination would last for years after its use was discontinued. _____

5. Perhaps as much as two-thirds of the DDT used by man may still be adrift and may still be working its way through the food chain up to man. _____

6. Even mother's milk has been found to contain DDT and the traces shown are often two or three times as high as the amount allowable for cow's milk. _____

7. The biological effects of DDT are magnified as it works its way up the food chain or as it is consumed by larger animals and higher forms of animal life. _____

8. For example, it may not harm a small fish but if a large fish eats a small fish that has ingested DDT, then the potency of insecticide may increase to the point of interfering with the large fish's reproductive cycle. _____

9. Of course, the food chain does not stop with the large fish nor does the effect of the DDT decline. _____

10. Fish-eating birds like the osprey suffer severely for this type of bird, like the bald eagle and the peregrine falcon, is gradually disappearing. _____

11. What the total effect of DDT on man will be is still unknown but the insecticide has been proved to cause tumors in mice and to affect memory and reaction time in man. _____

12. The use of DDT has declined since 1962 because of the adverse publicity and its decreasing effectiveness. _____

13. There are now 150 pests that are immune to DDT and doubtless many more varieties would be added to the list if widespread use of DDT were continued. _____

14. Although still exported, DDT is now banned for general use in the United States but our problems are far from solved because we still must deal with the effects of the DDT we have used in the past and, equally important, because we must develop a satisfactory replacement for controlling insects. _____

15. Today we use a variety of methods for controlling insects, such as trapping them with light and sound and planting insect-resistant crops but so far no method of control has proved as effective as DDT nor has any method proved as hazardous to man and his environment. _____

Commas after introductory clauses or phrases

NAME _____ SCORE _____

DIRECTIONS   Bracket introductory subordinate clauses and underline introductory phrases. After each introductory clause or phrase write a comma or a zero (0), according to whether you think the comma is desirable or not. Also write the comma or the zero in the blank at the right.

EXAMPLES

[When man alters his environment in any way,]there are bound
   to be some unpleasant ecological repercussions.   _____,_____
In achieving progress man often harms his environment.   _____0_____

1. Since man needs to travel for pleasure as well as for work
   impressive highway systems have been constructed.   _____

2. To modern man highways seem as necessary as food or water
   or air.   _____

3. However the highways that man constructs destroy nature
   and upset the ecological balance.   _____

4. During any year in this country alone we destroy over one
   million acres of trees with our highways.   _____

5. At the same time we eliminate a million acres of oxygen pro-
   ducers for our environment.   _____

6. While we make progress in one area of life we regress in another.   _____

7. Complicated though it may be the relationship between man
   and his environment must be understood if we are not to regress faster than we progress.   _____

8. Because everything in the environment is related to everything else we can never, as Barry Commoner says, "do merely
   one thing."   _____

9. Although the automobile may seem man's most trusted friend
   it is also one of his worst enemies.   _____

10. To maintain his trusted friend man pollutes the atmosphere
    with noxious gases and covers the land with concrete and
    asphalt.   _____

11. Impossible though it seems the highways in the United States would occupy the entire states of Massachusetts, Vermont, Connecticut, Rhode Island, and Delaware should their expanse be concentrated in a single area. _____

12. In Los Angeles the ratio of highway to land is astounding. _____

13. In fact 66 percent of the downtown area is covered by streets and parking lots. _____

14. Equally disturbing one-third of the Los Angeles area is paved with concrete and asphalt. _____

15. Whenever one discovers the enormity of the problem posed by the American automobile he naturally feels frustrated. _____

16. Of course Americans are not going to give up their cars. _____

17. In the nation's capital there is a lady who is fighting the automobile. _____

18. Believing in a mass transit system rather than individual automobiles she fights the development of the interstate highway systems in downtown Washington. _____

19. Certainly there are many others who feel that our country should build a mass transit system rather than more highways and parking lots. _____

20. At the moment these people represent a minority opinion, but as our country begins to look more and more like a giant parking lot their view may come to be shared by millions of others. _____

Commas between items in series and coordinate adjectives

NAME _____ SCORE _____

DIRECTIONS   Identify each series by writing *1, 2, 3,* etc., above the items and in the blanks at the right. Insert commas where they belong in the sentences and in the blanks at the right. Write *C* after each sentence that needs no revision.

EXAMPLES

The $\overset{1}{\text{well-fed,}}$ $\overset{2}{\text{well-clothed}}$ American produces an amazing amount of garbage each year.   <u>1, 2</u>

This garbage must be $\overset{1}{\text{burned,}}$ $\overset{2}{\text{covered over,}}$ or $\overset{3}{\text{disposed}}$ of in some other way.   <u>1, 2, 3</u>

1. Americans are accustomed to buying something today and discarding it tomorrow.   _____

2. A shiny new gadget of 1971 is a tarnished outmoded eyesore in 1972 or 1973.   _____

3. Thus, Americans buy and discard television sets refrigerators washing machines and cars at an unbelievable rate.   _____

4. Besides gadgets we pamper ourselves with the latest most exciting fashions.   _____

5. A fashionable lady cannot wear last year's green pants suit when chic red hot pants are the rage this year.   _____

6. Thus women discard short shorts for Bermuda shorts Bermuda shorts for long pants and long pants for hot pants.   _____

7. Today men, too, have regular rather drastic changes in wearing apparel which result in tall stacks of discards yearly.   _____

8. American know-how has developed disposable bottles cans napkins and diapers that must be discarded each day.   _____

9. With all the many outdated unusable and disposable items that man has, it is little wonder that each American discards about 5½ pounds of waste each day.   _____

10. Collectively over a year's time, Americans dispose of over 400 billion pounds of waste a year, a staggering incomprehensible figure that can be understood only when it is translated into other terms: we annually produce enough trash to fill the Panama Canal more than four times. _____

11. In 1968 the waste included, among other things, 2.6 billion bottles 30 million tons of paper 55 billion cans and 7 million automobiles. _____

12. Our country's annual trash bill is about 4.5 billion dollars a year, or more than we spend for any public service other than schools and roads. _____

13. Cities like New York and Chicago and San Francisco are facing a garbage crisis. _____

14. The old-standby methods for disposing of garbage—land-fill sites and outdated incinerators—are not the solution to our garbage dilemma. _____

15. Experts all over the world have turned their attention to the garbage problem and through careful planning and testing have offered several intriguing perhaps practical solutions. _____

16. Many experts believe that we can convert our garbage— papers cans bottles and even junk cars—into fertilizer. _____

17. In oversimplified terms, a giant machine would take in the garbage chomp it up and turn out bags of fertilizer. _____

18. Another scheme proposes that garbage be incinerated and the heat produced by the incineration process used as electric power. _____

19. Since modern techniques like these seem more expensive and more time-consuming than land-fill projects, many cities may hesitate to adopt them; thus the experts work especially hard to make their systems simple practical and profitable. _____

20. Hopefully one day soon garbage, instead of being a costly unpleasant nuisance, can be a profitable enterprise for cities. _____

Commas to set off nonrestrictive clauses or phrases   Exercise 12-4

NAME _____ SCORE _____

DIRECTIONS   Bracket adjective clauses and underline participial phrases. Set off nonrestrictive clauses or phrases with commas. In the blank at the right enter (1) a dash followed by a comma (–,) if the nonrestrictive element begins the sentence, (2) a dash preceded by a comma (,–) if the nonrestrictive element ends the sentence, or (3) a dash enclosed within commas (,–,) if the nonrestrictive element comes within the sentence. (4) Leave empty the blank at the right of each sentence with a restrictive clause or phrase.

EXAMPLES

Living in a day of "throwaways", we have become the world's worst litterbugs.   _–,_

Trash,[which should be deposited in litter barrels] is carelessly thrown to the ground.   _,–,_

Litter quickly accumulates, marring the appearance of our countryside.   _,–_

Today cans, bottles, and wrappers cover beaches and fields[that once were clean.]   _____

1. Once our country seemed like a wide expanse of space that we could never fill up.   _____

2. But today the space that once stretched seemingly everywhere is disappearing.   _____

3. Moving westward we have built businesses, apartment complexes, and housing developments to fill up our open spaces.   _____

4. And we have also filled up the open spaces with litter which now threatens to make our countryside look like a garbage dump.   _____

5. Everywhere we look—on television, in the newspapers and magazines, along roadways—there are signs that read, "Don't Litter."   _____

6. Having read the signs we promptly open our car windows and throw out our papers and bottles and cans along the highways.   _____

7. There are a few people who are conscientious enough to use litter baskets and litter barrels.   _____

8. But for every litter-conscious individual there are five others who show no concern for the environment. _____

9. Driving behind any car for five minutes or more we are likely to see the window go down and the garbage go out. _____

10. Now our beaches which once offered us sand and shells provide us with an assortment of bottle caps, broken glass, and jagged metal for us to cut our feet on. _____

11. Holiday weekends attracting more people than usual to the beaches and parks might well be called litter weekends. _____

12. On the Fourth of July weekend alone, Americans threw away enough litter to fill a basket that would rise as high as the Empire State Building. _____

13. A modern version of the Statue of Liberty shows the figure of the woman standing waist-deep in litter. _____

14. The famous statue holds in the place of a torch a garbage-can lid which the satirist suggests is a fitting symbol of our time. _____

15. Yet many of us closing our eyes to the ugliness around us continue to call our country "America the Beautiful." _____

16. Each year we spend tax dollars that could build 12,500 new schoolrooms for the pick-up of litter. _____

17. Men like Stewart Udall who has been active in the fight against pollution for many years remind us that "the earth is still our home." _____

18. Today every individual though frustrated by the ecological crisis can play a part in improving the environment. _____

19. He can eliminate the one litterbug who is closest at hand—himself. _____

20. In many communities today there are groups like "Those Who Care" and "The Citizens' Anti-Litter League" which meet weekly to organize clean-up campaigns. _____

Commas to set off parenthetical and nonrestrictive elements

NAME _____ SCORE _____

DIRECTIONS   Insert the commas needed to set off all parenthetical and nonrestrictive elements. In the space at the right enter (1) a dash followed by a comma (–,) to show a nonrestrictive or parenthetical element at the beginning of the sentence, (2) a dash enclosed within commas (,–,) to show a nonrestrictive or parenthetical element within the sentence, and (3) a dash preceded by a comma (,–) to show a nonrestrictive or parenthetical element at the end of the sentence.

1. Seeking an escape from the crowds and rush of the cities many thousands of people head for our national parks. _____

2. Once the national parks had a problem of too few people not too many. _____

3. The parks in an effort to attract tourists once had to spend money on publicity. _____

4. Today however publicity is unnecessary. _____

5. In 1969 over 164 million people visited our national parks a number that is really more than the parks can handle. _____

6. In most parks travel by car is difficult the traffic being bumper to bumper. _____

7. In the Smoky Mountains for example we may spend two hours advancing a few miles. _____

8. The town of Gatlinburg, Tennessee located in the foothills of the Smokies is as crowded during the tourist season as any large city. _____

9. People trying to get away from it all sometimes find themselves surrounded by everything they were trying to escape such as traffic jams, lines of people at restaurants, and noise. _____

10. Visiting a park of course does not have to be an experience in city living. _____

11. There are areas if one is not looking for all the conveniences of home where a person can go to be alone. _____

12. Strangely enough few people search out these areas. _____

13. The rangers at the Grand Teton National Park near Jackson, Wyoming claim that no more than 2 percent of the visitors get more than a few hundred yards from their cars. _____

14. The rangers you may be sure are not complaining about the lack of adventuresomeness of park visitors. _____

15. The remote nature trails like the highways winding through the parks could easily become overcrowded. _____

16. George B. Hartzog, Jr. the director of the National Park Service says that it is not the people who are clogging up the parks. _____

17. Rather he claims it is all the equipment the people bring with them that creates crowded conditions. _____

18. The campers have become a real headache to the park rangers mainly because of the great number who want camping space. _____

19. Many people want to see more camping sites constructed, but the park service generally resists further construction knowing that our parks could well become paved parking lots instead of wildlife refuges. _____

20. The National Park Service with its double purpose of preserving scenery and wildlife and making the parks available to an ever-increasing number of tourists faces what seems an impossible dilemma. _____

NAME _____ SCORE _____

DIRECTIONS   Insert all necessary commas, justifying each comma by writing above it (and in the space at the right) *a* (main clauses), *b* (introductory element), *c* (series or coordinate adjectives), or *d* (parenthetical element or nonrestrictive clause or phrase), in accordance with the principles explained in Section **12**.

EXAMPLE

In addition to the various pollutants we fill our environment with,   *b*

    we also upset the ecological balance by thoughtless killing of _____

    birds, reptiles, fish, and mammals.   *ccc*

1. Heeding all too well the admonition of Genesis 1:26 man has _____

   clearly established dominion over the fish of the sea the birds _____

   of the air the cattle and all the earth. _____

2. In fact man has gone far toward destroying all members of _____

   the animal kingdom including of course himself. _____

3. In the last 150 years man has increased his extermination of _____

   mammals alone by fifty-five-fold and if the killing continues _____

   at the present rate man may well destroy all 4,062 species of _____

   mammals within thirty years.

4. Even today there are 835 endangered species with more be- _____

   ing added each year.

5. In India where 40,000 tigers roamed in 1930 there are now _____

   only 2,500 left and the lion population currently estimated at _____

   175 has been depleted even more severely. _____

6. Australia a land of energetic sports-minded individuals has _____

   treated its animal population no better than India has. _____

7. Consequently animals like the kangaroo for which Australia _____

   is famous are fast disappearing as are koala bears Tasmanian _____

   wolves and emus. _____

8. Because Australians were not concerned about their wildlife _____

   in 1930 the government machine-gunned twenty thousand _____

   emus at one time.

9. In the United States too several species of wildlife have dis- _____

   appeared and many others are close to extinction. _____

10. The Eastern elk and the passenger pigeon once so plentiful in this country are now forever gone.
_____
_____

11. Other animals such as the alligator the Southern bald eagle and the ivory-billed woodpecker may be fated to join the growing list of species we will see no more.
_____
_____
_____

12. Although alligators are protected by law men continue to kill them for their skins only the belly portions of which are used.
_____
_____

13. As long as Americans want their expensive alligator belts handbags and shoes the poachers will continue to supply the skins.
_____
_____

14. The profit motive of course has led to the wholesale slaughter of animals like the alligator and the tiger but many other animals have been killed for whim or pleasure.
_____
_____

15. In Texas where it is not unusual to hear men speak of the fun they once had using whooping cranes for target practice many residents find it hard to believe that they should be fined for killing these giant birds even though the total whooping crane population is now estimated at approximately eighty.
_____
_____
_____
_____
_____

16. Perhaps no area has been more wasteful of its plant and animal life than Hawaii which has destroyed 36 percent of its wildlife species since Captain Cook's arrival 192 years ago.
_____
_____

17. Today in Hawaii one-half the insects one-half the land mollusks all the fresh-water fish and all the mammals are threatened with extinction.
_____
_____

18. Excessive hunting and fishing as well as the introduction of predators like rats and mongooses have resulted in the loss of more plants and animals in Hawaii in the last century than in all the other states combined.
_____
_____
_____

19. The news about wildlife is not all bad however because there are a few conservationists who work hard to counter some of the damage we have done.
_____
_____
_____

20. Through their efforts animals like the grizzly bear and the bison have been saved and endangered species like the whooping crane and the sea turtle are being restored.
_____
_____
_____

NAME _____ SCORE _____

DIRECTIONS   Insert all necessary commas, justifying each comma by writing above it (and in the space at the right) *a* (main clauses), *b* (introductory element), *c* (series or coordinate adjectives), or *d* (parenthetical element or nonrestrictive clause or phrase), in accordance with the principles explained in Section **12**.

1. Some people see no reason to be upset over the loss of _____
whooping cranes prairie dogs and alligators.   _____

2. Alligators they believe are not very pretty anyway and the _____
world is just as well off without their ugly scaly shapes.   _____

3. They are not impressed by the fact that the alligator one of _____
our oldest creatures is a link with the dinosaur of another age. _____

4. Valueless as the alligator may seem to many people it serves _____
a purpose other than satisfying scientific interest.   _____

5. In our environment everything is dependent on everything   _____
else and thus the loss of any species has an effect on others. _____

6. The loss of the ugly alligator for example endangers many _____
insects fish and amphibians.   _____

7. Enlarging the swamps where they live alligators provide deep _____
pools of water that serve as refuges for other animals during _____
droughts.

8. The hippopotamus another ugly animal also serves a useful _____
purpose a purpose that people recognized too late.   _____

9. Since the hippopotamuses seemed useless clumsy animals that _____
cluttered up the rivers in South Africa people shot them   _____
mercilessly.

10. Within a short time after the slaughter of the hippos schisto- _____
somiasis a debilitating disease began to increase at an alarm- _____
ing rate.

11. The hippos may have seemed useless to the people of South _____
Africa but they discovered otherwise after they had killed   _____
most of them off.

12. While bathing hippopotamuses keep river silt in motion and _____

when they finish with their baths they create irrigation ditches ＿＿＿＿＿

as they struggle up single file onto dry land. ＿＿＿＿＿

13. Without the hippos the rivers soon began to silt up and the ＿＿＿＿＿

excess water during heavy downpours had no ditches to run ＿＿＿＿＿

off into.

14. These changes in the environment resulted in a quick increase ＿＿＿＿＿

in schistosome-carrying snails which in turn spread the disease ＿＿＿＿＿

to human beings.

15. Now schistosomiasis is a health hazard in South Africa indeed ＿＿＿＿＿

as great a hazard in some areas as malaria once was. ＿＿＿＿＿

16. Again man learned that nature is very delicately balanced ＿＿＿＿＿

and that the balance is very easily upset.

17. Nature has supplied a vast assortment of species each neces- ＿＿＿＿＿

sary for the welfare of some other species.

18. The more varied the species in a given area the better the ＿＿＿＿＿

chance for an ecological balance because each species will ＿＿＿＿＿

keep some other in check.

19. Although the wolf is an enemy to the individual deer he acts ＿＿＿＿＿

as a friend to the species by preventing deer from overpopu- ＿＿＿＿＿

lating an area and dying from starvation. ＿＿＿＿＿

20. Thus every animal and plant regardless of how ugly or unim- ＿＿＿＿＿

portant it may seem has a function in nature to perform. ＿＿＿＿＿

13

Do not use superfluous commas.

Necessary commas indicate appropriate pauses and changes in voice pitch and thus help to clarify the meaning of a sentence. Unnecessary or misplaced commas, however, are false or awkward signals and often confuse the reader. Read the following sentences aloud to note how distinct pauses and changes in voice pitch indicate the need for commas.

> Boys, go to the gymnasium at two o'clock.   [Comma needed to indicate the distinct pause in direct address: see **12d**.]
> The boys go to the gymnasium at two o'clock.   [No commas needed]
>
> Helen enjoys tennis but ⊚ she cannot play well.   [Misplaced comma]
> Helen enjoys tennis, but she cannot play well.   [Comma needed before the coordinating conjunction, where the pause comes: see **12a**.]

If you have a tendency to use unnecessary commas, consider every comma you are tempted to use and omit it unless you can justify it by one of the principles treated under Section **12**. You may be helped also by the following suggestions.

13a   Do not use a comma to separate the subject from its verb or the verb from its object.

In the following sentences the encircled commas should be omitted.

> Americans abroad ⊚ are often very poor ambassadors for their own country. [Needless separation of subject and verb]
> He knew when he was only a boy ⊚ that politeness is important.   [Needless separation of verb and object]
> Some people believe ⊚ that "God Bless America" should be our national anthem.   [Indirect discourse: needless separation of verb and object]

Note: A comma before the verb sometimes makes for clarity when the subject is heavily modified.

> Americans who go to other countries expecting the same knowledge of the English language and the same air conditioning, ice water, and private baths found in hotels in the United States, are often very poor ambassadors for their own country.

13b   Do not use a comma to separate two words or two phrases joined by a coordinating conjunction.

In the following sentences the encircled comma should be omitted.

> The rise in crime is attributed to drugs ⊚ and organized crime.

I leaned over the parapet ⊙ and looked at the city spread out below me. [Compound predicate: *and* joins two verbs.]

He hoped to buy a new car ⊙ and to sell his old one. [*And* joins two infinitive phrases.]

13c   Do not use commas to set off words or short phrases (especially introductory ones) that are not parenthetical or that are very slightly so.

In the following sentences the encircled commas should be omitted.

Next week ⊙ I will go to a wedding ⊙ also.

Maybe ⊙ I should attend the meeting ⊙ too.

In the future ⊙ I expect to stay in school.

13d   Do not use commas to set off restrictive (necessary) clauses, restrictive phrases, or restrictive appositives.

In the following sentences the encircled commas should be omitted.

People ⊙ in glass houses ⊙ should not throw stones. [Restrictive phrase: no commas needed]

A man ⊙ who lives in a glass house ⊙ should not throw stones. [Restrictive clause]

My friend ⊙ Bill ⊙ threw a stone. [Restrictive appositive]

13e   Do not use a comma before the first or after the last item of a series.

Andrea did a study of famous women such as ⊙ Cleopatra, Dido, and Josephine. [Needless comma before first item of a series]

The sensuous, strong-willed ⊙ Cleopatra attracted both Julius Caesar and Mark Antony. [Needless comma after last adjective in a series]

Main and subordinate clauses

NAME _____ SCORE _____

DIRECTIONS Bracket all subordinate clauses in the following correctly punctuated sentences. In the first blank indicate the type of subordinate clause: adjective (*adj*), adverb (*adv*), or noun (*n*). In the second blank indicate by rule number and letter (see Sections **12** and **13**) why a comma is or is not used with the clause.

EXAMPLE

	Clause	*Rule*
One ill effect of overcrowding[that we often over-look]is nervous tension.	*adj*	*13d*

1. Whenever animals are confined in great numbers to a small area, they develop all kinds of nervous disorders.

2. Sometimes, in fact, they die if they are subjected to extreme overcrowding.

3. Anyone who has studied the devastating effects of overpopulation on the lemmings, small arctic rodents, must think seriously about population control.

4. If a population explosion occurs among the lemmings, then many of the species go mad and literally kill themselves.

5. Because their glands malfunction as a result of overcrowding, they experience a sudden change in the level of their blood sugar.

6. Damage to brain cells, which results from the change in blood sugar, causes many of the lemmings to commit suicide.

7. "But man, who is far above the lemming in intelligence, is not likely to commit suicide because of the population explosion," many people respond.

8. There is evidence that man is adversely affected by overcrowding.

9. Suicide rates among human beings are highest in areas where the population is most over-crowded. _____ _____

10. The incidence of suicide is also very high among the old, who often feel unneeded and unwanted. _____ _____

11. To be happy, a man must feel that his existence is meaningful. _____ _____

12. That overcrowding robs a man of his sense of worth cannot be denied. _____ _____

13. How valuable can a man feel when he is daily shoved around by masses of people? _____ _____

14. One stands in line for almost everything today, even for the experiences which supposedly bring pleasure. _____ _____

15. "Hurry up and wait" has become a motto that we live with daily. _____ _____

16. Although the consequences of overcrowding may not be as apparent for man as they are for the lemming, they may indeed be as serious. _____ _____

17. Ulcers, heart diseases, and mental disorders, which afflict ever increasing numbers, are all partly traceable to the stresses produced by overcrowding. _____ _____

18. Another symptom of overcrowding, which is becoming more apparent each year, is insensitivity to death and suffering. _____ _____

19. Because the world now has too many people, we are no longer affected by reports of major disasters. _____ _____

20. Insensitivity to suffering and death is sometimes appallingly illustrated in cities like New York, where a girl received no help from the dozens of people watching her being murdered. _____ _____

Superfluous commas; all uses of the comma

NAME _____ SCORE _____

DIRECTIONS Explain each comma used properly by writing above it (and in the space at the right) *a* (main clauses), *b* (introductory element), *c* (series or coordinate adjectives), or *d* (parenthetical element or nonrestrictive clause or phrase), in accordance with the principles explained in Section **12**. If you cannot justify the use of the comma by one of these principles, indicate that the comma is superfluous by circling it and by entering an encircled comma in the space at the right.

EXAMPLE

Indeed,*ᵇ* overpopulation,*ᵈ* a problem most people have only recently   *bd*

begun to recognize,*ᵈ* is the main source of the majority of our   *d*

other⦶ ecological difficulties.   ⦶

1. Pollution of the air and water, loss of privacy, overcrowding   _____
   of cities, highways, and parks are all largely, a result of the   _____
   population explosion.

2. For many years, this country improved, as a result of popu-   _____
   lation growth, but today the increasing population is a detri-   _____
   ment, rather than, an advantage.   _____

3. Because people got accustomed to having large families, to   _____
   perform the many jobs on the farms, we have continued to   _____
   have children, even though many children are no longer nec-   _____
   essary, or even desirable.   _____

4. Romanticizing the notion of the large family, many parents   _____
   continue to have four or more children, regardless of their   _____
   ability to support them economically or emotionally.   _____

5. Everyone recognizes, that it costs money to rear children   _____
   properly, but few people, who plan large families, realize just   _____
   how much the cost is.

6. One estimate, which comes from the Institute of Life Insur-   _____
   ance, suggests that $23,800 is required to rear a child to the   _____
   age of eighteen, a sum that does not include the cost of a col-   _____
   lege education.

7. When there are many children in the family, there, quite nat-   _____
   urally, is not enough money, to provide all that the parents   _____
   have hoped for their children.

8. Another expense of a different type, is frequently overlooked. _____

9. Parents, who have too many children, are drained emotionally _____
   as well as financially.

10. Children from small families, those with fewer than four chil- _____
    dren, prove to be brighter, more creative, and more inde- _____
    pendent, than children from large families. _____

11. Surprisingly enough, they even grow taller, and bigger than _____
    children from large families.

12. The studies that document these findings, are based on fam- _____
    ilies with similar incomes, not poor, large families matched _____
    against small, middle-class families. _____

13. A famous, classic study, by the Institute of Mental Health, _____
    shows that closely spaced babies from large families, tend to _____
    be lethargic right after birth, and their lack of responsiveness _____
    is still evident, at nursery-school age. _____

14. Apparently the mothers, who did not have time to recover _____
    physically between births, were also depleted emotionally by _____
    their many children, perhaps more than they realized. _____

15. Overburdened emotionally, they had less love and attention _____
    to give their new babies, who were thus deprived of what, _____
    other than food, they needed most. _____

16. Studies have shown, too, that beatings and other kinds of _____
    abuse, while not the rule, are more common in large families _____
    than in small ones.

17. It is obvious, then, that the parents, as well as the children, _____
    suffer, when the family is too large. _____

18. In fact, parents, with four or more children are more likely _____
    to become patients in mental hospitals, than parents with _____
    fewer children.

19. Having little time, money, and energy for their own pur- _____
    suits, parents of large families are deprived of activities, that _____
    they could enjoy, if they did not have so many children. _____

20. Of course, life is easier for rich parents who have many chil- _____
    dren than it is for poor ones, but studies show, that the psy- _____
    chological ill effects of large families apply to the rich, as well _____
    as to the poor.

14

Use the semicolon (a) between two main clauses not joined by a coordinating conjunction (*and, but, or, nor, for*) and (b) between coordinate elements containing commas. (Use the semicolon only between parts of equal rank.)

In speaking, the pause required for the semicolon is almost as full as that for a period; in fact, the semicolon is sometimes called a weak period. The pause test can help you place the semicolon as well as the comma, but you should rely chiefly on your knowledge of the structure of the sentence.

14a   Use the semicolon between two main clauses not joined by a coordinating conjunction or between two main clauses joined by a coordinating conjunction but containing a great deal of internal punctuation.

PATTERN   MAIN CLAUSE; MAIN CLAUSE

It is not the good that one takes such care to conceal; it is the vicious and unworthy that most people sweep under the rug.

We have enjoyed learning to maneuver a canoe, a sailfish, and a sunfish; but we have had more fun with our catamaran than with any other type of boat.

Note: Use a semicolon between two main clauses joined by a conjunctive adverb or a transitional phrase.

PATTERN   MAIN CLAUSE; $\left\{ \begin{array}{c} \textit{conjunctive adverb} \\ \textit{or} \\ \textit{transitional phrase} \end{array} \right\}$ MAIN CLAUSE

There was a fascination for him in studying hard; nevertheless, he was aware of a vague unhappiness.

Passing the bar examination took all his thoughts; as a result, finding the girl faded into the background.

14b   Use the semicolon to separate a series of equal elements which themselves contain commas.

At camp Susan signed up for swimming, which everybody had to take; crafts, which she enjoyed the most; and riding, which she really needed to improve.

Caution: Use the semicolon between parts of equal rank only, not between a clause and a phrase or a main clause and a subordinate clause.

PARTS OF EQUAL RANK   The rattler was coiled to strike; the biology class approached it with caution.   [Two main clauses]

PARTS OF UNEQUAL RANK   Because the rattler was coiled to strike, the biology class approached it with caution.   [Subordinate clause and main clause separated by a comma]

15

Use the apostrophe (a) to indicate the possessive case—except for personal pronouns, (b) to mark omissions in contracted words or numerals, and (c) to form certain plurals.

15a   Possessives—except for personal pronouns

(1) For words (singular or plural) not ending in an s or z sound, add the apostrophe and s ('s).

> The man's hat, the boy's shoes   [Singular]
> Men's hats, women's dresses   [Plural]
> One's hat, anybody's coat   [Indefinite pronouns—singular]

(2) For singular words ending in an s or z sound, add the apostrophe and s ('s) for words of one syllable. For words of more than one syllable, add only the apostrophe unless the second s is to be pronounced.

> James's book, Moses' commands, Sartoris's dream

(3) For plural words ending in an s or z sound, add only the apostrophe.

> Ladies' hats (hats for ladies), boys' shoes (shoes for boys)

(4) Compounds or nouns in joint possession show the possessive in the last word only.

> My father-in-law's house, someone else's hat, Helen and Mary's room

Caution: Do not use the apostrophe with the personal pronouns (*his, hers, its, ours, yours, theirs*) or with the relative-interrogative pronoun *whose*. Note especially that *it's* means *it is*.

> *It's* cold today.   [*It is* cold today.]
> Virtue is *its* own reward.

15b   Omissions in contractions

> Can't, didn't, he's (he is), it's (it is), you're (you are), o'clock (of the clock), the class of '55 (1955).

Notice that the apostrophe is placed exactly where the omission occurs.

15c   Plurals of letters, figures, symbols, and words referred to as words

> Congreve seldom crossed his *t*'s, his 7's looked like 9's, and his *and*'s were usually *&*'s.

Semicolons

NAME _____ SCORE _____

DIRECTIONS In the following sentences insert an inverted caret (V) between main clauses and add semicolons as needed. In the blank at the right copy the semicolon and the word immediately following. Write C if the sentence is correct. (Bracket any subordinate clause that appears incidentally.)

EXAMPLES

The world's population continues to grow at an alarming
rate⌄last year alone we added two million to the popula-
tion of the United States.   _; last_

The United States is not as heavily populated[as other countries are,]but we are suffering from overcrowding.   _C_

1. The world's population must be stabilized, otherwise we will reach a point where there is standing room only on this planet.   _____

2. At the present rate of population increase, for example, there will be 60 million billion people within nine hundred years, each person will have one-hundredth of a square yard of space to occupy.   _____

3. The doubling of population has changed unbelievably during the course of man's history, it has progressed from 1,000,000 years doubling time to 1,000 years, to 200 years, to 80 years, and finally to 37 years.   _____

4. Some people feel that science can supply the needs of our ever increasing population, that science can provide the extra food and space needed.   _____

5. But science cannot add land when we fill up all that we have, neither can science produce natural resources when we deplete those we have.   _____

6. It is true that the famines predicted for the 1970's may have been delayed by improved agriculture practices, however, the so-called green revolution cannot forestall famine for long if our population continues to expand. _____

7. It seems unlikely that we will be able to use the moon

or other planets to absorb our excess population thus we must make do with the space we have on earth. _____

8. Besides, even if we could live on the other planets in our solar system, we would, in a very short time, overpopulate them, indeed we could fill all the planets to earth's density of population within two hundred years. _____

9. Nature has various ways of controlling population: reduction of litter size, parental neglect, as witnessed in the lion family, genetic deterioration, in which the gene pool of an entire species may be sapped by the weak and deficient members, and even mass suicide, frighteningly demonstrated by the lemmings. _____

10. Geneticists see genetic deterioration and mass suicide due to stress as real threats to the human species, consequently, they propose that man stabilize his population rather than force nature to do so for him. _____

11. There are other ways—war, famine, and pestilence—by which human population has traditionally been stabilized, but all of these methods, which man has worked hard to eliminate, are cruel and, in fact, unnecessary. _____

12. Even with statistics before them, Americans desire three or more children, a number that will result in a population that our country cannot adequately support. _____

13. Parents in many other countries are even less concerned about their spiraling population than Americans are, in India, for instance, the women who seek help from family planning centers are usually over thirty and already have six children. _____

14. In general, American parents limit their families more than Indian parents do, however, American families require more from the land than do Indian families. _____

15. Although we are only one-fifteenth of the world's population, we require over one-half of the world's raw materials to maintain our standard of living, and, in living as we do, we are many times harder on the land, air, and water than the population of India is. _____

NAME _____ SCORE _____

DIRECTIONS   In the following sentences insert an inverted caret (V) between main clauses and add semicolons as needed. In the blank at the right copy the semicolon and the word immediately following. Write *C* if the sentence is correct.

1. Population experts recommend that parents have no more than two children, with this limitation it will still require eighty years for the population of the United States to stabilize itself.   _____

2. There has never been a country which achieved a high level of education that did not decrease its birth rate, conversely, nations of illiterate and poorly educated people have proved unable to control their populations.   _____

3. Education is clearly one of the key steps to a stabilized population, but education in itself is not the total answer to our problem.   _____

4. As Joseph Wood Krutch, a famous American naturalist, has pointed out, the population of the United States has been steadily increasing despite improved education and widespread knowledge of methods of birth control, therefore we have to look elsewhere for the cause of our population explosion.   _____

5. Krutch believes the cause is rooted in man's instinct, in other words, man's intellect, though trained, is unable to control his instinct.   _____

6. Man knows that large families are undesirable, however, his basic instinct to reproduce is more powerful than his intellect.   _____

7. There are encouraging signs, however: 70 percent of children from large families are limiting their own families, many young adults are adopting children after they have had one or two of their own, and a few young adults, rather than having any children of their own, are

turning entirely to adoption for establishing their families.

8. Many Americans support legislative programs that would encourage small families, for example, tax incentives for having few children instead of many.

9. Most Americans favor voluntary population control, a few support enforced population control.

10. Believing that we will delay too long to limit our population voluntarily, a number of people feel that government control, while not desirable, is inevitable if we are to stabilize our population.

11. Americans can set an example for the rest of the world, by stabilizing our own population, we can show other countries the advantages of population control.

12. A decrease in population means a decrease in many other ecological problems, such as pollution, depletion of natural resources, and excessive noise.

13. Each person born is more than just a birth statistic, he represents 56,000,000 gallons of water, 21,000 gallons of gasoline, 250 cans a year to be disposed of, and 3 pounds of air pollutants a day.

14. He is someone to be fed, clothed, and educated, he is someone to crowd parks, airports, and restaurants, he is someone to create garbage, air pollutants, and noise.

15. Each person, then, is a vital statistic in many ways, some good and some bad, thus the decision to reproduce another person is a national and world concern as well as an individual one.

16. The development of a baby's talents cannot be achieved through mass production, rather it requires the energy, time, and attention of his parents.

Apostrophes

NAME _____ SCORE _____

DIRECTIONS   In the sentences below insert all necessary apostrophes. In the blanks at the right enter each word to which you have added an apostrophe. Be careful not to add needless apostrophes. If the line is correct, write *C* in the blank.

EXAMPLE

Today ecology is everyone's concern.   *everyone's*

1. In past times the Joneses and the Smiths too often said,   _____
   "Ecology is someone elses concern, not ours."   _____

2. The Jones family could destroy a section of land, then   _____
   move on and claim other land as theirs.   _____

3. The Smiths garbage could be left uncovered because no   _____
   one would see it except them and occasional visitors to   _____
   their home.   _____

4. Today, though, one mans land is, in a sense, everyones   _____
   land, and anyones litter is an eyesore for everyone else   _____
   to see.   _____

5. In the 1970s the population is too concentrated for in-   _____
   dividuals to live in isolation; todays people are forced   _____
   to be neighbors to others.   _____

6. John Donnes statement that no man is an island has   _____
   never been truer, and his warning that the bells tolling   _____
   for another persons death is really a tolling for your   _____
   own death is an apt slogan for the conservationists.   _____

7. The conservationists writings warn us that a death bell   _____
   is tolling for all mankind.   _____

8. Our countrys future, as well as the worlds future, de-   _____
   pends on everyones heeding ecologys warning bell.   _____

9. Its too late to cover our ears and pretend not to hear, to _____
   say, "Ill get by even if the world doesnt."   _____

10. Typically each person turns to his neighbor and asks,   _____
    "Whos to blame for the ecological catastrophe?"   _____

11. We find it easy to say its the industrialists fault and the   _____
    scientists problem.   _____
12. But really the fault is ours and the problem is ours.   _____
13. Mans lack of reverence for the earth is to blame, and, as   _____
    one ecologist points out, that lack of reverence "goes a   _____
    long way back."   _____
14. Weve taken many years to get to our current plight, but   _____
    we dont have many years to get out of it.   _____
15. Man, whose intelligence supposedly distinguishes him   _____
    from the other animals, has traditionally waited until   _____
    problems have become almost insoluble before he has   _____
    become concerned.   _____
16. Hopefully, the lyricists words "The times, they are   _____
    a-changing" apply to youths concern for the total en-   _____
    vironment.   _____
17. There have always been men who, like the nineteenth   _____
    centurys Henry David Thoreau, could read the signs of   _____
    the times.   _____
18. Thoreau, one of Americas first naturalists, looked at his   _____
    fellow citizens thoughtless destruction of the forests and   _____
    cried, "Thank God, they cannot cut down the clouds."   _____
19. A modern naturalists cry is that we can and we are cut-   _____
    ting down the clouds.   _____
20. Perhaps the Joneses and the Smiths children will act on   _____
    the warnings of the naturalists of the twentieth century.   _____

Apostrophes

NAME _____ SCORE _____

DIRECTIONS   In the sentences below insert all necessary apostrophes. In the blanks at the right enter each word to which you have added an apostrophe. Be careful not to add needless apostrophes. If the line is correct, write *C* in the blank.

1. Many ecologists prediction of a major famine during the   _____
   1970s does not seem far-fetched when one considers   _____
   how many of the worlds people today are starving.   _____

2. Approximately one-third of the earths people are either   _____
   malnourished or undernourished.

3. Its difficult to say how many people die each year from   _____
   hunger, because starvations toll is exacted in many ways.   _____

4. Hungers allies include diseases like pneumonia and flu,   _____
   which prey on the bodys weakened condition.   _____

5. Indias population is, of course, more subject to starva-   _____
   tion than the United States.   _____

6. Only about ten million of that countrys 530 million peo-   _____
   ple eat the foods they need for an adequate diet.   _____

7. We shouldnt feel complacent about adults and childrens   _____
   diets in this country either.   _____

8. Americas hungry number about ten million, an unbe-   _____
   lievable figure for the worlds richest country.   _____

9. Many Americans in both the cities and rural areas eat   _____
   dog food, laundry starch, and even dirt to make their   _____
   stomachs feel full.   _____

10. One frequently hears stories of children eating paint   _____
    scrapings because their parents income is too little to   _____
    provide the food their bodies crave.   _____

11. Malnutrition in babies and expectant mothers affects the   _____
    minds development as well as the bodys.   _____

12. The IQs of children from severely impoverished families   _____
    rarely develop as they should because of the infants   _____
    protein deficiency.

13. Everyones welfare is affected by the poors plight be- _____
cause undernourished people often do not have the _____
energy even to improve their own living conditions, _____
much less contribute to societys improvement. _____

14. Once again someone elses welfare directly affects our _____
own.

15. The Presidents minimum payment to a family of four _____
provides for a dinner like this: one helping of collard _____
greens and rice and one cup of tea or Kool-Aid. _____

16. The bad effects of such a diet are readily apparent; yet _____
many of our nations poor can never expect anything _____
better unless drastic steps are taken. _____

17. Population control is, of course, necessary because ex- _____
hausting the lands carrying capacity means starvation _____
for people in all countries. _____

18. Various plans have been presented for increasing the _____
food supply, but many of our agriculturists proposals _____
seem impractical after weve thought about them awhile. _____

19. The seas resources have long been pointed to as our _____
hope for feeding our escalating population; however, _____
now it is widely recognized that the various oceans ca- _____
pacities for agricultural development are rather limited. _____

20. Most experts plans for farming the oceans are based on _____
the inshore areas, where man is likely to have some suc- _____
cess but also where pollutions done its worst damage. _____

16

Use quotation marks to set off all direct quotations, some titles, and words used in a special sense. Place other marks of punctuation in proper relation to quotation marks.

16a   Direct quotations

Enclose all direct (but not indirect) quotations within double quotation marks (" "). Use single quotation marks (' ') for a quotation within another quotation. Remember that quotation marks must be used in pairs.

> "I feel," said Nan, "that the statement 'All men are created equal' is the cornerstone of liberty."
> She said, "Equality is a basic right."   [Direct quotation]
> She said that equality is a basic right.   [Indirect quotation]

Note: Long prose quotations and three or more lines of poetry are indented from the body of the text and single-spaced. Quotation marks are not used.

16b   Minor titles

Titles of short stories, articles from magazines, short poems, and chapters from books are regularly enclosed in quotation marks.

> "Lousy Wednesday" is a chapter in John Steinbeck's novel *Sweet Thursday*.

16c   Words used in a special sense

Words used in a special sense are sometimes enclosed in quotation marks.

> An eminent virologist has said that a "good" virus is hard to find.

16d   Position of quotation marks in relation to other marks

(1) The period and the comma are always placed *within* the quotation marks.

> "Play ball," the umpire shouted. "The rain is over."

(2) The colon and the semicolon are always placed *outside* the quotation marks.

> The test covered "Chicago"; next week we begin *Abraham Lincoln*.

(3) The dash, the question mark, and the exclamation point are placed within the quotation marks when they apply only to the quoted matter; they are placed outside when they apply to the whole sentence.

> He shouted, "Where are my record albums?"
> What is meant by "the generation gap"?

17

Use the period, the question mark, the exclamation point, the colon, the dash, parentheses, and brackets in accordance with accepted usage.

17a Use the period after declarative and mildly imperative sentences, after indirect questions, and after most abbreviations.

Jon fainted.   Come quickly.   Ask Dr. Oldham if he can come.

17b Use the question mark after direct (not after indirect) questions.

Did you hear my new record?   I asked if you heard my new record.

17c Use the exclamation point after emphatic interjections and after phrases, clauses, or sentences to express surprise or other strong emotion.

Horrors!   The car crashed!   How terrible!

17d Use the colon after a formal introductory statement to direct attention to what follows.

The famous passage reads: [Here the colon introduces a long quotation. Commas are generally used to introduce a short quotation.]
There were three items on her grocery list: milk, eggs, and bacon. [Note that a dash may be used instead of the colon here.]

17e Use the dash to mark a sudden break in thought, to set off a summary, or to set off a parenthetical element that is very abrupt or that has commas within it.

Many dances of the 1960's—the twist, the frug, and the swim—emphasize the separation of the sexes.

17f Use parentheses (1) to enclose figures or letters when used for enumeration, as in this rule, and (2) to set off parenthetical, supplementary, or illustrative matter.

Parentheses set off parts loosely joined to the sentence and minimize them.

Bette (pronounced "Bet") is an actress.

17g Use brackets to set off editorial comments in quoted matter.

One of Shakespeare's most famous lines is, "My [Macbeth's] way of life / Is fall'n into the sere, the yellow leaf."

NAME _____ SCORE _____

DIRECTIONS   In the sentences below insert all needed quotation marks. In the blanks at the right enter these marks and the first and last word of each quoted part. Include other marks of punctuation used with the quotation marks, placed in their proper positions. Do not enclose indirect quotations, but write *C* in the blank at the right to indicate that the sentence is correct without quotation marks.

EXAMPLES

Garrett Hardin has said, "We can never do merely one thing."

           "We – thing."

1. Once you understand the problem, Barry Commoner explains, you find it's worse than you ever expected. _____

2. Many ecologists have said that the world is doomed regardless of what we do. _____

3. Others claim, There is still time to save ourselves if we act immediately. _____

4. Stephanie Mills, in an article entitled The Beginning of a Magazine and the End of the World, has made several memorable statements. _____

5. At one point in the essay she comments, We believe that peace on earth and peace with earth are one and the same. _____

6. Have you seen Paul Ehrlich's list of man's inalienable rights? an ecologist friend of mine asked. _____

7. The last right listed by Ehrlich is worded in this way: The right to have grandchildren. _____

8. There is a parody of America the Beautiful that includes many frightening images. _____

9. One stanza reads:
America, America, thy birds have fled from thee;
Thy fish lie dead by poisoned streams from sea
   to fetid sea. _____

10. Most ecologists believe we must change our pattern of life if we are to survive. _____

11. The Age of Effluence, an article in *Time* Magazine, points out, At this hour, man's only choice is to live in harmony with nature, not conquer it. _____

12. The article recommends, among other things, that man learn to recycle waste as nature does. _____

13. How about a beer container that is something like a pretzel? Or a soft-drink bottle that, when placed in the refrigerator, turns into a kind of tasty artificial ice? the article asks. _____

14. What do you think of the article's statement, The perfect container for mankind is the edible ice-cream cone? the lecturer asked his students. _____

15. At a recent seminar on the environment, the speaker reminded the teen-agers in his audience, Ecology is an in thing today. _____

16. Even comic strips like Miss Peach and Peanuts stress ecology. _____

17. And many songs about ecology, like What Have They Done to the Rain? have become popular. _____

18. The word ecology is on everyone's lips. _____

19. But history teaches us that fads too often die out. _____

20. Stephanie Mills warns us, If we fail to turn the fad into direct action, we die. . . . _____

Commas and other marks of punctuation

NAME _____ SCORE _____

DIRECTIONS   In the sentences below insert all needed marks of punctuation. Also enter these marks (only the marks you have added) in the same order in the blanks at the right. Be careful, both in the sentences and in the blanks at the right, to place quotation marks in proper relation to other marks of punctuation. Be prepared to justify all commas, whether added by you or not.

EXAMPLE

Several years ago Norman Cousins, the editor of the *Saturday Review,* wrote an editorial entitled "The Noise Level is Rising."
　　　　　　　　　　　　　　　　　　　　　　　,
　　　　　　　　　　　　　　　　　　　　　　　, " "

1. In the nineteenth century the Romantic poets and essayists namely Wordsworth Shelley Emerson and Thoreau wrote about the mystical experience one could have in nature.　_____ _____ _____

2. One essential requirement for this experience was quietness a silence of all things except natures voice.　_____ _____

3. When Wordsworth or Emerson stood on a high mountain or in a deep forest he was separated from the sounds of society then he could adopt "the wise passiveness" a mood of quietness that Wordsworth described in his short poem Expostulation and Reply.　_____ _____ _____ _____ _____

4. Emerson said that at a time like this when the spirit leads man on he becomes to use the essayists own words a transparent eyeball.　_____ _____ _____

5. It is during these quiet moments in nature when man undergoes the transcendental experience that he comes to understand the mysteries of the universe.　_____ _____ _____

6. Wordsworth describes the experience in this way
   While with an eye made quiet by the power
   Of harmony, and the deep power of joy,
   We see into the life of things.　_____ _____ _____ _____

7. A later poet W. B. Yeats also spoke of the effect of quietness on the spirit of man in The Lake Isle of Innisfree And I shall have some peace there, for peace comes dropping slow, /　_____ _____ _____

Dropping from the veils of the morning to where the cricket _____

sings. . . . _____

8. Men like Yeats Wordsworth and Emerson you might also be _____

interested in reading the accounts of Thoreaus and Shelleys _____

experiences in nature were able to get away from the noises _____

of the world they could find places near their own homes _____

where they could be entirely alone. _____

9. Is it possible for me to be alone today? one might well ask. _____

And if so where can I go to find quiet? Where is a place that _____

is not bombarded by noise? _____

10. Once isolated spots even the national parks are now filled _____

with adults with children and consequently with noise. _____

11. If a person goes high onto a mountaintop or deep into a forest _____

today he is still likely to see another person or at the very _____

least to hear the noises of another persons gun or airplane or _____

car.

12. After searching for solitude one almost inevitably comes to _____

this conclusion quietness is a state unknown to modern man. _____

13. Thus there is another pollution problem that troubles still an- _____

other of mans senses his sense of hearing. _____

14. The noise level as Norman Cousins and others have pointed _____

out is indeed rising and one wonders how much more noise _____

man can tolerate.

15. Some of the noise man actually seeks out such as the many _____

decibels of sound from a rock band he pays to hear other _____

noise such as traffic construction and talking is thrust upon _____

him.

16. Noise is everywhere even in ones home the radio or television _____

is blaring and the vacuum cleaner and washing machine are _____

roaring not to mention the chattering and shouting of other _____

members of the family.

DIRECTIONS   In the sentences below insert all needed marks of punctuation. Also enter these marks (only the marks you have added) in the same order in the blanks at the right. Be careful, both in the sentences and in the blanks at the right, to place quotation marks in proper relation to other marks of punctuation. Be prepared to justify all commas, whether added by you or not.

1. Noise acoustics experts define noise as "meaningless sound" _____
   begins to affect the body when the level reaches seventy _____
   decibels an amount usually generated by traffic on a quiet _____
   city street.

2. A decibel as you probably know is a unit for measuring sound _____
   it is the lowest amount of sound a man can hear. _____

3. With each rise in decibels above the mark of seventy the _____
   body is further upset as demonstrated by such bodily reac- _____
   tions as muscle contractions sudden releases of adrenalin and _____
   quickened heartbeat.

4. Each day one is exposed to a variety of noisemakers above _____
   the seventy-decibel range for example an ordinary truck or _____
   sports car releases 90 decibels a loud power mower 107 deci- _____
   bels electric guitars in a rock band 114 decibels and a jet _____
   plane at takeoff 150 decibels. _____

5. A persons eardrums are remarkably resistant to loud irritating _____
   noises at eighty-five decibels the muscles behind the eardrums _____
   relax.

6. A person then hears less and his eardrums because the mus- _____
   cles are relaxed do not break. _____

7. After the intense noise has decreased to the eighty-five–decibel _____
   range the muscles again tighten and the individual's hearing _____
   is restored to normal at least almost to normal. _____

8. One never quite regains his former level of hearing thus con- _____
   tinuous exposure to loud noises eventually results in perma- _____
   nent hearing impairment.

9. A surprising number of Americans suffer from some degree _____

of hearing impairment eighteen million a larger number than   _____

experience all other types of disabilities combined.   _____

10. Other parts of the body are also affected by noise the nervous   _____

    system the heart the digestive system.   _____

11. A person who suffers from cardiac trouble is particularly af-   _____

    fected by loud noise it can result in his having an anginal   _____

    seizure.

12. Needless to say there are other less serious results anxiety loss   _____

    of sleep and perhaps even ulcers from continuous exposure to   _____

    intense sound.

13. W. H. Ferry a close observer of the noise level has written   _____

    We are more a dinful than a sinful nation.   _____

14. What can be done about the rising noise level a person asks   _____

15. Certain devices for reducing the noise level have been pro-   _____

    duced for example there are motors designed to run quietly.   _____

16. These motors usually cost slightly more than their noisy coun-   _____

    terparts but a 5 percent additional payment for a quiet-running   _____

    motor is much cheaper than a doctors or a psychiatrists bill.   _____

17. Certain parts of the country like the San Francisco Bay area   _____

    are particularly noise-conscious and they are taking definite   _____

    steps to ensure their citizens right to quietness.   _____

18. In San Francisco for example a new rapid-transit system is   _____

    being constructed to reduce the number of cars on downtown   _____

    streets.

19. Using electronic devices to check the volume of sound Cali-   _____

    fornia is keeping a close watch on its traffic noise and is even   _____

    designing freeways with noise inhibitors in mind.   _____

20. In Dortmund Germany several years ago the people invoked   _____

    a law that reads Public health is above any economic consid-   _____

    eration and today Dortmund is a quiet pleasant city one that   _____

    is no longer threatened by a noise plague.

Review of all marks of punctuation

NAME _____ SCORE _____

DIRECTIONS   Use in sentences of your own, with proper capitalization and punctuation, each of the elements listed below. In the space at the right show all marks of punctuation used (except periods to end sentences).

EXAMPLE

a word, or words, in apposition (**12d**)   _____ , , _____

Barry Commoner, a famous ecologist, has spoken for many years about the various threats to our environment.

1. two coordinate adjectives modifying the same noun (**12c**)   _____

2. a restrictive clause (**12d**)   _____

3. two main clauses not joined by a coordinating conjunction (**14a**)   _____

4. a series of three verbs (**12c**)   _____

5. a parenthetical phrase (**12d**)   _____

6. a direct question (**17b**)   _____

7. two main clauses joined by a coordinating conjunction (**12a**)   _____

8. a summary within a sentence (**17e**)   _____

9. an introductory adverbial clause (**12b**)   _____

10. a nonrestrictive clause (**12d**)   _____

11. a list of items at the end of a sentence (**17d**)   ————

12. a quotation interrupted by *he replied* (**12d**)   ————

DIRECTIONS   Use in sentences of your own, with proper capitalization and punctuation, each of the elements listed below. Enter in the space at the right the specific word form, word, or title (properly punctuated) that you are required to use in the sentence.

EXAMPLE

the title of a long play   *The Effect of Gamma Rays on Man-in-the-Moon Marigolds*

The Effect of Gamma Rays on Man-in-the-Moon Marigolds is a play about a mother's influence on her children.

13. a foreign word or phrase (Section **10**)   ————

14. the possessive of *it* (**15a**)   ————

15. the contraction of *it is* (**15b**)   ————

16. the possessive plural of *mother-in-law* (**15a**)   ————

17. the title of a magazine article (**16b**)   ————

18. the title of a book (Section **10**)   ————

19. the possessive plural of *woman* (**15a**)   ————

20. the title of a short poem (**16b**)   ————

Spelling and Hyphenation   sp 18

18

Spell every word according to established usage as shown by a good dictionary.

Mastering the words you misspell as they come to your attention day by day is undoubtedly one of the best methods of improving your spelling. This method, which was explained in the Preface, will be continued throughout the course. But you may get a special insight into your difficulties by analyzing the list of words you have misspelled. Once you have determined your particular difficulties, you may help to overcome them by learning to apply the rules designed to help you. You should certainly not burden yourself with those rules which, by analysis of your spelling, you find not applicable to your needs. As a basis for the exercises in this section, the common reasons for misspelling are listed below.

18a   Mispronunciation

(1) Do not omit a letter: *arctic, family, used*

(2) Do not add a letter: *athlete, film, hindrance*

(3) Do not change a letter: *accurate, prejudice*

(4) Do not transpose letters: *cavalry, hundred, prefer*

18b   Confusion of words similar in sound

Distinguish between words of similar sound and spelling.

allusion, illusion; berth, birth; dual, duel; lose, loose

If your errors fall chiefly under **18a** and **18b**, you are not actually a poor speller; your misspellings are due to your insufficient knowledge of pronunciation and the exact meanings of words.

18c   Failure to distinguish prefix from root; changes in adding suffixes

(1) Add the prefix to the root without doubling or dropping letters.

dis- (prefix) + appear (root) = disappear   [One *s*]
im- + mortal = immortal   [Two *m*'s]
un- + necessary = unnecessary   [Two *n*'s]

(2) Drop the final e before a suffix beginning with a vowel but not before a suffix beginning with a consonant.

bride + -al = bridal; fame + -ous = famous
care + -ful = careful; entire + -ly = entirely

Exceptions: *due, duly; awe, awful; hoe, hoeing; singe, singeing.* After *c* or *g* the final *e* is retained before suffixes beginning with *a* or *o: notice, notice-able; courage, courageous.*

(3) When the suffix begins with a vowel (-*ing*, -*ed*, -*ence*, -*ance*, -*able*), double a final single consonant if it is preceded by a single vowel and comes in an accented syllable. (A word of one syllable, of course, is always accented.)

mop, mo**pp**ing; run, ru**nn**ing
con·fer′, con·fer′red   [Final consonant in the accented syllable]
ben′e·fit, ben′e·fited   [Final consonant not in the accented syllable]
need, needed   [Final consonant not preceded by a single vowel]

Note how important this rule is in forming the present participle and the past tense of verbs.

(4) Except before -*ing*, final y preceded by a consonant is changed to *i* before a suffix.

defy + -ance = defiance; happy + -ness = happiness
modify + -er = modifier; modify + -ing = modifying

Final *y* preceded by a vowel is usually not changed before a suffix.

annoy + -ed = annoyed; array + -ing = arraying

Exceptions: *pay, paid; lay, laid; say, said; day, daily.*

18d   Confusion of *ei* and *ie*

If you confuse these letters in your spelling, learn and follow these two rules: (1) When the sound is *ee* (as in *see*), write *ei* after *c* (*receipt, ceiling*) and *ie* after any other letter (*relieve, priest*). (2) When the sound is other than *ee*, usually write *ei: eight, their, reign.*

Exceptions: *either, neither, financier, leisure, seize, species, weird.*

18e   Forming the plural

Form the plural by adding *s* to the singular (*boy, boys*) but by adding *es* if the plural makes an extra syllable (*bush, bushes*).

18f   Hyphenated words

In general, use the hyphen **(1)** between words serving as a single adjective before a noun (a *know-it-all* expression), **(2)** with compound numbers from twenty-one to ninety-nine, **(3)** with prefixes or suffixes for clarity (*re-creation* of the scene), and **(4)** with the prefixes *ex-* (meaning "former"), *self-*, *all-*, and the adjective *-elect* (*mayor-elect*).

General spelling list

Exercise 18-1

NAME ______________________________ SCORE ____________

DIRECTIONS Study as necessary the following words in groups of fifty (or as directed by your instructor) and use each word in a sentence (written out on a separate sheet of paper). Copy in your Individual Spelling List on pages 179–80 every word that you tend to misspell, following carefully the directions on page 179.

This spelling list is drawn from Dean Thomas Clark Pollock's study of 31,375 misspellings in the written work of college students.[1]

The Hundred Words Most Frequently Misspelled

In the list below the most troublesome letters for all words are in boldface. Asterisks indicate the most frequently misspelled words among the first hundred. Only American spellings are given.

[I]

1. accommodate
2. achievement
3. acquire
4. all right
5. among
6. apparent
7. argument
8. arguing
9. belief *
10. believe *
11. beneficial
12. benefited
13. category
14. coming
15. comparative
16. conscious
17. controversy
18. controversial
19. definitely
20. definition
21. define
22. describe
23. description
24. disastrous
25. effect
26. embarrass
27. environment
28. exaggerate
29. existence *
30. existent *
31. experience
32. explanation
33. fascinate
34. height
35. interest
36. its, it's
37. led
38. lose
39. losing
40. marriage
41. mere
42. necessary
43. occasion *
44. occurred
45. occurring
46. occurrence
47. opinion
48. opportunity
49. paid
50. particular

[II]

51. performance
52. personal
53. personnel
54. possession
55. possible
56. practical
57. precede *
58. prejudice
59. prepare
60. prevalent
61. principal
62. principle
63. privilege *
64. probably
65. proceed
66. procedure
67. professor
68. profession
69. prominent
70. pursue
71. quiet
72. receive *
73. receiving *
74. recommend
75. referring *
76. repetition
77. rhythm
78. sense
79. separate *
80. separation *
81. shining
82. similar *
83. studying
84. succeed
85. succession
86. surprise
87. technique
88. than
89. then
90. their *
91. there *
92. they're *
93. thorough
94. to, * too, * two *
95. transferred
96. unnecessary
97. villain
98. woman
99. write
100. writing

The Next 550 Words Most Frequently Misspelled

[III]

101. absence
102. abundance
103. abundant
104. academic
105. academically
106. academy
107. acceptable

---

[1] Thomas Clark Pollock and William D. Baker, *The University Spelling Book* (Englewood Cliffs, N.J.: Prentice-Hall, 1955), pp. 6–12. See also Thomas Clark Pollock, "Spelling Report," *College English*, 16 (Nov. 1954), 102–09.

108. acceptance
109. accepting
110. accessible
111. accidental
112. accidentally
113. acclaim
114. accompanied
115. accompanies
116. accompaniment
117. accompanying
118. accomplish
119. accuracy
120. accurate
121. accurately
122. accuser
123. accuses
124. accusing
125. accustom
126. acquaintance
127. across
128. actuality
129. actually
130. adequately
131. admission
132. admittance
133. adolescence
134. adolescent
135. advantageous
136. advertisement
137. advertiser
138. advertising
139. advice, advise
140. affect
141. afraid
142. against
143. aggravate
144. aggressive
145. alleviate
146. allotted
147. allotment
148. allowed
149. allows
150. already

[IV]

151. altar
152. all together

153. altogether
154. amateur
155. amount
156. analysis
157. analyze
158. and
159. another
160. annually
161. anticipated
162. apologetically
163. apologized
164. apology
165. apparatus
166. appearance
167. applies
168. applying
169. appreciate
170. appreciation
171. approaches
172. appropriate
173. approximate
174. area
175. arise
176. arising
177. arouse
178. arousing
179. arrangement
180. article
181. atheist
182. athlete
183. athletic
184. attack
185. attempts
186. attendance
187. attendant
188. attended
189. attitude
190. audience
191. authoritative
192. authority
193. available
194. bargain
195. basically
196. basis
197. beauteous
198. beautified
199. beautiful

200. beauty

[V]

201. become
202. becoming
203. before
204. began
205. beginner
206. beginning
207. behavior
208. bigger
209. biggest
210. boundary
211. breath
212. breathe
213. brilliance
214. brilliant
215. Britain
216. Britannica
217. burial
218. buried
219. bury
220. business
221. busy
222. calendar
223. capitalism
224. career
225. careful
226. careless
227. carried
228. carrier
229. carries
230. carrying
231. cemetery
232. certainly
233. challenge
234. changeable
235. changing
236. characteristic
237. characterized
238. chief
239. children
240. Christian
241. Christianity
242. choice
243. choose
244. chose

245. cigarette
246. cite
247. clothes
248. commercial
249. commission
250. committee

[VI]

251. communist
252. companies
253. compatible
254. competition
255. competitive
256. competitor
257. completely
258. concede
259. conceivable
260. conceive
261. concentrate
262. concern
263. condemn
264. confuse
265. confusion
266. connotation
267. connote
268. conscience
269. conscientious
270. consequently
271. considerably
272. consistency
273. consistent
274. contemporary
275. continuously
276. controlled
277. controlling
278. convenience
279. convenient
280. correlate
281. council
282. counselor
283. countries
284. create
285. criticism
286. criticize
287. cruelly
288. cruelty
289. curiosity

290. curious	335. endeavor	380. generally	425. indispensable
291. curriculum	336. enjoy	381. genius	426. individually
292. dealt	337. enough	382. government	427. industries
293. deceive	338. enterprise	383. governor	428. inevitable
294. decided	339. entertain	384. grammar	429. influence
295. decision	340. entertainment	385. grammatically	430. influential
296. dependent	341. entirely	386. group	431. ingenious
297. desirability	342. entrance	387. guaranteed	432. ingredient
298. desire	343. equipment	388. guidance	433. initiative
299. despair	344. equipped	389. guiding	434. intellect
300. destruction	345. escapade	390. handled	435. intelligence
	346. escape	391. happened	436. intelligent
[VII]	347. especially	392. happiness	437. interference
301. detriment	348. etc.	393. hear	438. interpretation
302. devastating	349. everything	394. here	439. interrupt
303. device, devise	350. evidently	395. heroes	440. involve
304. difference		396. heroic	441. irrelevant
305. different	[VIII]	397. heroine	442. irresistible
306. difficult	351. excellence	398. hindrance	443. irritable
307. dilemma	352. excellent	399. hopeless	444. jealousy
308. diligence	353. except	400. hoping	445. knowledge
309. dining	354. excitable		446. laboratory
310. disappoint	355. exercise	[IX]	447. laborer
311. disciple	356. expense	401. hospitalization	448. laboriously
312. discipline	357. experiment	402. huge	449. laid
313. discrimination	358. extremely	403. humorist	450. later
314. discussion	359. fallacy	404. humorous	
315. disease	360. familiar	405. hundred	[X]
316. disgusted	361. families	406. hunger	451. leisurely
317. disillusioned	362. fantasies	407. hungrily	452. lengthening
318. dissatisfied	363. fantasy	408. hungry	453. license
319. divide	364. fashions	409. hypocrisy	454. likelihood
320. divine	365. favorite	410. hypocrite	455. likely
321. doesn't	366. fictitious	411. ideally	456. likeness
322. dominant	367. field	412. ignorance	457. listener
323. dropped	368. finally	413. ignorant	458. literary
324. due	369. financially	414. imaginary	459. literature
325. during	370. financier	415. imagination	460. liveliest
326. eager	371. foreigners	416. imagine	461. livelihood
327. easily	372. forty	417. immediately	462. liveliness
328. efficiency	373. forward	418. immense	463. lives
329. efficient	374. fourth	419. importance	464. loneliness
330. eighth	375. friendliness	420. incidentally	465. lonely
331. eliminate	376. fulfill	421. increase	466. loose
332. emperor	377. fundamentally	422. indefinite	467. loss
333. emphasize	378. further	423. independence	468. luxury
334. encourage	379. gaiety	424. independent	469. magazine

470. magnificence	515. parliament	560. religion	605. sufficient
471. magnificent	516. paralyzed	561. remember	606. summary
472. maintenance	517. passed	562. reminisce	607. summed
473. management	518. past	563. represent	608. suppose
474. maneuver	519. peace	564. resources	609. suppress
475. manner	520. peculiar	565. response	610. surrounding
476. manufacturers	521. perceive	566. revealed	611. susceptible
477. material	522. permanent	567. ridicule	612. suspense
478. mathematics	523. permit	568. ridiculous	613. swimming
479. matter	524. persistent	569. roommate	614. symbol
480. maybe	525. persuade	570. sacrifice	615. synonymous
481. meant	526. pertain	571. safety	616. temperament
482. mechanics	527. phase	572. satire	617. tendency
483. medical	528. phenomenon	573. satisfied	618. themselves
484. medicine	529. philosophy	574. satisfy	619. theories
485. medieval	530. physical	575. scene	620. theory
486. melancholy	531. piece	576. schedule	621. therefore
487. methods	532. planned	577. seize	622. those
488. miniature	533. plausible	578. sentence	623. thought
489. minutes	534. playwright	579. sergeant	624. together
490. mischief	535. pleasant	580. several	625. tomorrow
491. moral	536. politician	581. shepherd	626. tragedy
492. morale	537. political	582. significance	627. tremendous
493. morally	538. practice	583. simile	628. tried
494. mysterious	539. predominant	584. simple	629. tries
495. narrative	540. preferred	585. simply	630. tyranny
496. naturally	541. presence	586. since	631. undoubtedly
497. Negroes	542. prestige	587. sincerely	632. unusually
498. ninety	543. primitive	588. sociology	633. useful
499. noble	544. prisoners	589. sophomore	634. useless
500. noticeable	545. propaganda	590. source	635. using
	546. propagate	591. speaking	636. vacuum
[XI]	547. prophecy	592. speech	637. valuable
501. noticing	548. psychoanalysis	593. sponsor	638. varies
502. numerous	549. psychology	594. stabilization	639. various
503. obstacle	550. psychopathic	595. stepped	640. view
504. off		596. stories	641. vengeance
505. omit	**[XII]**	597. story	642. warrant
506. operate	551. psychosomatic	598. straight	643. weather
507. oppose	552. quantity	599. strength	644. weird
508. opponent	553. really	600. stretch	645. where
509. opposite	554. realize		646. whether
510. optimism	555. rebel	**[XIII]**	647. whole
511. organization	556. recognize	601. strict	648. whose
512. original	557. regard	602. stubborn	649. yield
513. pamphlets	558. relative	603. substantial	650. you're
514. parallel	559. relieve	604. subtle	

NAME _____ SCORE _____

DIRECTIONS   With the aid of your dictionary write out each of the following words by syllables, mark the position of the main accent, and pronounce the word correctly and distinctly. In your pronunciation avoid any careless omission, addition, change, or transposition.

EXAMPLE   similar   *sim'i·lar*

1. environment _____

2. perspiration _____

3. escape _____

4. athlete _____

5. hundred _____

6. hindrance _____

7. undoubtedly _____

8. preparation _____

9. library _____

10. surprise _____

11. sophomore _____

12. mathematics _____

13. literature _____

14. veteran _____

15. suffrage _____

16. recognize _____

17. mischievous _____

18. miniature _____

19. hungry _____

20. despair _____

21. temperament _____

22. manufacturers _____

23. cemetery _____

24. quantity _____

25. villain _____

26. children _____

27. competitive _____

28. experiment _____

29. desirous _____

30. incidentally _____

Confusion of words similar in sound

NAME _____ SCORE _____

DIRECTIONS In the following sentences strike out the spelling or spellings within parentheses that do not fit the meaning and write the correct spelling in the blank at the right. Consult your dictionary freely.

EXAMPLE

(Your, ~~You're~~) efforts in ecology's behalf are important. _____*Your*_____

1. (Their, There, They're) are several organizations that play significant (roles, rolls) in the fight to save our environment. _____

2. Zero Population Growth tries to (altar, alter) society's outdated (beliefs, believes) about the value of large families. _____

3. Planned Parenthood / World Population (to, too, two) reminds us of the results of continuing our present (coarse, course) of population growth. _____

4. The Wilderness Society is one of the groups (who's, whose) purpose is to preserve the few (cites, sights, sites) of uninhabited land left. _____

5. Friends of the Earth is (quiet, quite) successful in its use of (ingenious, ingenuous) techniques to remind people of the necessity for population control. _____

6. (An, And) the National Audubon Society encourages society not to (loose, lose) interest in its plant and animal life. _____

7. The time has (passed, past) when people laugh at the (prophecies, prophesies) of organizations like the Sierra Club. _____

8. We no longer consider books on ecology (irrelevant, irreverent) to our survival; in fact, we feel that a (thorough, through) knowledge of environmental studies is a necessity. _____

9. The (affect, effect) of environmental organizations and publications on governmental policy is now generally (accepted, excepted). _____

10. (Weather, Whether) we belong to an environmental-concern group or not, we must make ecology one of our (principal, principle) interests. _____

Adding suffixes

NAME _____ SCORE _____

DIRECTIONS   In the blank at the right enter the correct spelling of each word with suffix added. In the middle blank state the reason for the spelling entered.

EXAMPLES

bride + -al   *Drop final e before a vowel.*   *bridal*

care + -ful   *Retain final e before a consonant.*   *careful*

due + -ly   *Exception*   *duly*

drop + -ing   *Before a vowel, double a final single consonant preceded by a single vowel and coming in an accented syllable.*   *dropping*

droop + -ing   *A final single consonant preceded by two vowels is not doubled.*   *drooping*

defy + -ance   *Except before -ing, final y preceded by a consonant is changed to i.*   *defiance*

annoy + -ed   *Final y preceded by a vowel is usually not changed.*   *annoyed*

1. try + -es   _____   _____

2. employ + -ed   _____   _____

3. change + -ing   _____   _____

4. begin + -ing   _____   _____

5. true + -ly   _____   _____

6. lone + -liness   _____   _____

7. nine + -ty   _____   _____

8. leap + -ing   _____   _____

9. notice + -able   _____   _____

10. boundary + -es   _____   _____

11. arrange + -ment   _____   _____

12. control + -able   _____   _____

13. enjoy + -able   _____   _____

14. arouse + -ing   _____   _____

NAME _____ SCORE _____

DIRECTIONS   With the aid of your dictionary fill in the blanks in the following words by writing *ei* or *ie*. In the blank preceding the word state the rule applicable. Write *Exception* in the blank preceding any word that is an exception to the rule.

EXAMPLES

When the sound is ee, write ei after c.
When the sound is ee, write ie after any letter other than c.
When the sound is other than ee, usually write ei.
Exception

dec_ei_ve
bel_ie_ve
th_ei_r
_ei_ther

1. _____ perc___ve

2. _____ rel___ve

3. _____ r___gn

4. _____ v___n

5. _____ n___ce

6. _____ l___sure

7. _____ c___ling

8. _____ f___nd

9. _____ h___ght

10. _____ repr___ve

11. _____ gr___ve

12. _____ st___n

13. _____ rec___pt

14. _____ l___ge

15. _____ sl___gh

16. _____ bel___f

17. _____ consc___nce

18. _____ misch___f

19. _____ conc___ve

20. _____ ach___ve

Good Use   g 19
Exactness   e 20
Wordiness   w 21
Omission of Necessary Words   ^ 22

19

Learn how to use the dictionary; select appropriate words.

One of the best investments a student makes is the purchase of a good desk dictionary. Unabridged dictionaries, like *Webster's Third New International*, can be found in the library, but everyday use requires a smaller, abridged dictionary. A desk dictionary is used for more purposes than finding the correct spelling of a word. To name only a few others, it tells the student how to pronounce a word like *harass;* what a word like *fancy* originally meant, as well as the various meanings it has today; what the principal parts for an irregular verb like *sing* are; and what usage label may be given for a word like *poke*.

Dictionaries vary in their listing of usage labels; some, in fact, have dropped most labels. Once the student has secured a good desk dictionary, he should study the introductory matter to learn the attitude his dictionary takes toward usage labels as well as the order in which the meanings of words are listed—that is, in order of historical development or of common usage.

19a   Standard English and labeled words   Most words (or meanings of words) in the dictionary are unlabeled—that is, they have no label such as *Slang* or *Dialectal* and are accordingly in good and general use throughout the English-speaking world. Unlabeled words (or unlabeled meanings of words) make up what is called the standard or formal English vocabulary and may be used freely as they fit the writer's needs. But words entered in the dictionary with a label should be used with caution.

19b   Informal words   Informal words (labeled *Informal* or *Colloquial* by most dictionaries) are appropriate to the conversation of cultivated people and to informal writing but tend to bring a discordant note into formal writing.

> INFORMAL   I played hooky, but I didn't get away with it.
> FORMAL   I stayed away from school, but I was discovered.

19c   Slang   Slang is a special type of colloquial language that is often objectionable because it tends to become trite and vague.

> SLANG   This is a *crummy* apartment.
> STANDARD   This is a *shabby* (OR *inferior*) apartment.

19d   Dialectal words   Dialectal words (labeled *Dialectal* or assigned to some locality, such as *Southern U.S.*) should normally be avoided because they are often meaningless outside the limited region where they are current.

DIALECTAL   It was *boughten.*
STANDARD   It was *not homemade.*   OR   It was *bought at the store.*

19e   Vulgarisms or illiteracies   Vulgarisms (labeled *Illiterate*) are the non-standard expressions of uneducated people and are usually not listed in the dictionary.

NONSTANDARD   *They's* no one here but me.
STANDARD   *There's* no one here but me.

19f   Obsolete or archaic words   Obsolete words are no longer in general use, but they are listed as an aid in reading our older literature.

19g   Technical words   Technical words (given such labels as *Law, Architecture, Nautical*) are peculiar to one group or profession and should be avoided in addressing a general audience or in writing for the general reader.

20

Find the exact, idiomatic, fresh word.

WRONG WORD   The explosion *effected* her hearing.
RIGHT WORD   The explosion *affected* her hearing.
UNIDIOMATIC   It was a difficult task he *set to* me.
IDIOMATIC   It was a difficult task he *set for* me.
TRITE   This is *a shining example of* good writing.
BETTER   This is good writing *at its best.*

21

Avoid wordiness.

WORDY   The reason why I dread the summer is because my room is hot.
BETTER   I dread the summer because my room is hot.
REPETITIOUS   There are *various and sundry* theories about education.
BETTER   There are *various* theories about education.

22

Omit no word essential to the meaning.

INCOMPLETE   The French class is over and the students leaving.
COMPLETE   The French class is over and the students *are* leaving.

NAME _____ SCORE _____

The full title, the edition, and the date of publication of my dictionary are as follows:

_____

1. Abbreviations   Where are abbreviations found? _____
Write out the meaning of each of the abbreviations following these sample entries:

pollute, *v.t.*, *L* _____   earth, *n.*, *OE* _____

lief, *adj.*, *Obs.* _____   know-it-all, *adj.*, *Colloq.* _____

2. Spelling and Pronunciation   Write out by syllables each of the words listed below, and place the accent where it belongs. Consult your dictionary. With the aid of the diacritical marks (in parentheses immediately after the word) and the key at the bottom of the page or in the introductory matter, determine the preferred pronunciation (the first pronunciation given) of each word. Then pronounce each word correctly several times. Be prepared to pronounce each word in class.

harass _____   status _____

short-lived _____   advertisement _____

Write the plurals of the following words:

passer-by _____   estuary _____   octopus _____   species _____

Determine which of the following words should be written with a hyphen and rewrite those that need a hyphen.

nonconformist _____   longrange _____   coexist _____

3. Derivations   The derivation, or origin, of a word (given in brackets) often furnishes a literal meaning that throws much light on the word. For each of the following words give (a) the source—the language from which it is derived, (b) the original word or words, and (c) the original meaning.

	Source	*Original Word and Meaning*
ecology	____	_____
endemic	____	_____
effluent	____	_____

4. Meanings   Usually words develop several different meanings. (Note that *Webster's Seventh New Collegiate Dictionary* and *Webster's New World Dictionary of the American Language* list meanings 1, 2, etc., in order of historical development.) How many meanings are listed for the following words?

in, *prep.* _____   time, *n.* _____   when, *conj.* _____

real, *adj.* _____   hold, *v.* _____   off, *adv.* _____

5. Special Labels   Words (or certain meanings of words) may have such precautionary or explanatory labels as *Archaic, Colloquial, Dialectal, Obsolete, Slang, Nautical,* or *Law.* What label or special usage do you find for one meaning of each word below?

business, *n.* _____   fair, *v.i.* _____   binary, *adj.* _____

in, *n.* _____   dope, *v.* _____   down, *n.* _____

6. Synonyms   Even among words with nearly the same essential meaning, one word usually fits a given sentence more exactly than any other. To show exact shades of meaning, some dictionaries treat in special paragraphs certain groups of closely related words. What synonyms are specially differentiated in your dictionary along with the following words?

command, *v.* _____

explain, *v.* _____

7. Capitalization   Of the following words rewrite those that should be capitalized.

biology _____   negro _____   koran _____

darwinism _____   capitalism _____   philistinism _____

8. Grammatical Information   Note that many words may serve as two or more parts of speech. Classify each of the following words (according to the first listing in the dictionary) as *v.i., v.t., n., adj., prep.,* or *conj.* Give the principal parts of each verb.

interest _____   away _____   effect _____

lie _____   show _____   clean _____

9. Miscellaneous Information   Answer the following questions by referring to your dictionary and be prepared to tell in what part of the dictionary the information is located.

In what year was Henry David Thoreau born? _____

What is the area of the Gulf of Mexico? _____

Who was Jean Jacques Rousseau? _____

NAME _____ SCORE _____

DIRECTIONS   Consult your dictionary to determine whether the italicized words, as used in the following sentences, conform to formal English usage. If the word, with the meaning it has in its particular sentence, is labeled in any way, enter this label (such as *Informal* or *Slang*) in the blank at the right. If the word is not labeled, write *Formal* in the blank. Go over your answers in class to compare the usage labels of various dictionaries.

EXAMPLE

There are *lots of* things one can do to improve the environment.   *Colloquial*

1. Almost no student today is *disinterested* in ecology. _____

2. He asks the experts, "*Ain't* there something I can do to help?" _____

3. And he is told that there is *considerable* he can do to improve the environment. _____

4. The earth needs every *guy's* help. _____

5. *Sith* litter is one of our country's obvious ecological problems, an individual can pledge *his'n* efforts to combat litter. _____

6. He can also be *plenty* helpful by keeping his disposable containers to a minimum. _____

7. If he will *stick to* returnable bottles instead of throwaway cans, he can help to alleviate the excess garbage *fix* we are in. _____

8. Since colored paper is *liable* to pollute water, he can use white tissues and toilet paper. _____

9. He can keep *abreast* of the facts about laundry detergents and gasolines. _____

10. If he *suspicions* that he uses more electricity and water than necessary, he can try *real* hard to eliminate any wastefulness. _____

11. In *raising* his children, he can be careful to teach them to be good stewards of their *propriety*, the earth. _____

12. He can refuse to *set* around and allow his air and water to become more polluted. _____

Good use (formal English usage)

NAME _____ SCORE _____

DIRECTIONS   In the following sentences cross out any word or phrase not appropriate in formal writing. In the blank at the right enter the formal English equivalent. Write *C* in the blank opposite each sentence in which all words are used in accordance with formal writing.

EXAMPLE

One ~~can't~~ hardly avoid the topic of ecology.   *can*

1. Today it is difficult to get off of the subject of ecology.   _____

2. When a person talks about the great amount of people he sees wherever he goes, he is talking about an ecological problem.   _____

3. In ordinary conversation people talk about the things that once were different to what they are today.   _____

4. Someone speaks of the days when he went in the woods to be alone.   _____

5. Another says he remembers the time when a autumn day was clear and the air was fresh.   _____

6. Still another claims he once could of caught good game fish in the lake near his home.   _____

7. Someone else suggests that the air is inferior than the air he remembers breathing a few years ago.   _____

8. When one opens the daily paper, he reads about people which are threatened by mercury poisoning or radioactive materials or toxic gases.   _____

9. One cannot avoid thinking about ecology without he closes his eyes to the sights around him.   _____

10. Being as the roadways are lined with billboards, junk car lots, and litter, a person cannot escape ecological problems even when he goes for a leisurely drive with his family.   _____

11. Irregardless of where he goes, one is confronted with traffic and noise.   _____

12. It is no wonder, then, that people look back and compare the ecological conditions of past times with conditions today.   _____

Correct and exact words

NAME _____ SCORE _____

DIRECTIONS   Cross out the inappropriate word or words. Let the correct, exact word stand in the sentence, and enter it in the space at the right. Consult your dictionary freely.

EXAMPLE

What kind of living conditions will people be forced to (accept, ~~except~~) in the year 2000?   *accept*

1. Paul Ehrlich has written a (prophecy, prophesy) for the year 2000 which he has framed as an annual report to the President.   _____

2. It is (quiet, quite) interesting, though sometimes horrifying, to read Ehrlich's predictions.   _____

3. He reports a high (incidence, incidents) of leukemia and dwarfism as a result of a nuclear reactor disaster in 1981.   _____

4. Also, a high rate of genetic damage can be (attributed, contributed) to the release of radioactive material in the atmosphere during the 1970's.   _____

5. Ehrlich estimates that sixty-five million Americans have died from starvation but that another major famine has been (averted, diverted), unless climatic conditions change unexpectedly.   _____

6. Ehrlich theorizes (to, too, two) that 125 million Americans died as a result of an epidemic of what he calls *Marburgirrus B.*   _____

7. The (epic, epoch) when this virus threatened to destroy the world's population Ehrlich calls the period of the Great Die-Off.   _____

8. Ehrlich's report predicts that agricultural progress is (preceding, proceeding) after the disaster years of the 1980's.   _____

9. His (advice, advise) to the President is that continued government assistance to agriculture should result in an American diet comparable to that of 1960.   _____

10. He reports that the nonrenewable resource crisis has been delayed for one hundred years as a result of the decrease in population, but he (councils, counsels) the

President that international planning for resource husbandry must go ahead.

11. Not (everyone, every one) of Ehrlich's predictions is unpleasant.

12. For example, he reports that the quality of both air and water has (succeeded, surpassed) what it was in 1960.

13. Most of the disasters Ehrlich (accounts, recounts) are a result of the release of radioactive material into the atmosphere.

14. It seems that the general population during the 1960's and 1970's was (incredible, incredulous) about the long-range effects of radioactive fallout.

15. Radioactive fallout (lead, led) to many major disasters, like susceptibility to *Marburgirrus B* and a change in weather patterns.

16. One (implies, infers) from Ehrlich's report that the prevention of radioactive fallout is the major concern of the 1970's.

17. Ehrlich urges the world to become (conscious, conscience) of the disasters he foresees for the 1970's and 1980's.

18. Lest the world (loose, lose) nearly four billion lives during these years, Ehrlich recommends that people take action.

19. He feels it is (contemptible, contemptuous) for people to continue to allow the environment to deteriorate.

20. He hopes that his report about what awaits man in the near future will (elicit, illicit) concern for the ecologists' suggestions for improving our environment.

Correct and exact words

NAME _____ SCORE _____

DIRECTIONS In the following sentences strike out each word used inappropriately and write the correct or exact word or words in the blank at the right. Write *C* in the blank at the right of each sentence in which all words are used appropriately.

EXAMPLE

Prior ~~than~~ World War II the total supply of radium in the world was about ten grams.

to

1. In passed times man's experience with radioactive materials was slight.

2. Before the development of the atomic bomb during World War II, man had released only small quantities of radioactive material into the atmosphere.

3. But between 1948 and 1962 man preceded to experiment with nuclear fission.

4. One affect of this experimentation was the release of enough strontium 90 into the atmosphere to equal one billion grams of radium.

5. When one compares ten grams of radium to one billion grams, he realizes how significant the increase in nuclear fallout was after World War II.

6. Between 1956 and 1964 the appraisal of the biological consequences of fallout was remarkably altered, as evidenced by a comparison of the official statements of Presidents Eisenhower and Johnson.

7. In 1956 President Eisenhower formerly stated that the continued testing of H-bombs posed no threat to the health of mankind.

8. But by 1964 President Johnson acclaimed the dangers of nuclear testing.

9. He said radioactive fallout was a menace to the health of adults, children, and unborn babies, that it was poisoning the very air that man must breath.

10. The nuclear test ban treaty of 1963 recognized the dangers of the presents of nuclear fallout and prevented further testing in the atmosphere by the United States

and the Soviet Union, the principal powers then engaged in testing.

11. Again, though, man may of decided to change his course of action too late.

12. The biologists which evaluate the effects of strontium 90 on the body are not optimistic.

13. There reports show that such hazards of nuclear testing as cancer and genetic damage were grossly underestimated for too long.

14. These kind of miscalculation are all too prevalent in man's history.

15. Usually man purposes to take a course of action before be evaluates the effects of that action.

16. But its incorrect to assume that man does not learn from his mistakes, as the nuclear test law attests.

17. Today the public's reaction to the SST shows that technological progress can no longer remain unquestioned; weather right or wrong about the SST, man has begun to consider the long-range effects of technology.

18. Man no longer automatically ascents to the notion that technological advances are always advisable.

19. In fact, we are experiencing a period of history when man questions all formerly accepted principles and beliefs.

20. Perhaps this questioning will lead to a new type attitude toward man's environment.

NAME _____ SCORE _____

DIRECTIONS   Bracket needless words in each of the following sentences. For each sentence needing no further revision, write *1* in the blank at the right; for other sentences write *2* in the blank and make the needed revision.

EXAMPLES

There are various[and sundry]books on ecology.   *1*

~~The reason why~~ ǿne should read books on ecology ~~is learning~~ *to learn*

about the threats to his environment.   *2*

1. Rachel Carson was a woman who pioneered in ecological studies.   _____

2. She wrote *Silent Spring* in order that she might awaken people to the dangers of insecticide poisoning.   _____

3. In the book it tells about a spring when no birds sang.   _____

4. The reason that the robins disappeared from many areas of the country was that the elms were being heavily sprayed with DDT.   _____

5. The robin population was affected indirectly for one simple reason: the reason was that they ate earthworms that had stored DDT in their bodies.   _____

6. The earthworm's favorite food is the leaf litter from elms that they like better than anything else.   _____

7. Consequently, DDT reached the robins that fed on the infected earthworms for this reason.   _____

8. Robins eat many earthworms a day, and they eat as many as an earthworm a minute.   _____

9. As few as eleven infected earthworms can kill a robin and cause the bird to die.   _____

10. Not each and every robin died as a result of DDT poisoning.   _____

11. Many robins faced extinction for another reason: this was because of sterility induced by the absorption of DDT.   _____

12. One of the saddest pictures Rachel Carson paints in her book is a robin sitting on its eggs faithfully for twenty-one days

without their hatching, and this is one of the saddest pictures in the book. _____

13. Almost simultaneously at the same time people in various parts of the country began to notice a scarcity of robins. _____

14. At the Michigan State University campus an ornithologist who studies bird life might once have seen 370 robins, but in 1957 he could find only two or three dozen. _____

15. In 1958 the ornithologist could not find a single fledgling robin on the campus, and this is even more depressing. _____

16. Thus efforts to control Dutch elm disease almost destroyed not only the robin population but it also proved disastrous to many other species of earthworm-eating birds. _____

17. The robins are used as an example by Rachel Carson in order to illustrate the plight of all living things. _____

18. It was largely because of Rachel Carson's horrifying account of a silent spring without birds that was the reason that the American public became interested in ecology. _____

19. In the 1960's students all over the country were reading *Silent Spring* and they were discussing it. _____

20. *Silent Spring* was published in 1962, and it is not a recent book, but it is still one of the most influential ecological studies. _____

NAME _____ SCORE _____

DIRECTIONS In the following sentences insert the words that are needed to complete the sense and write these words in the blanks at the right.

EXAMPLE

Rachel Carson's *The Sea Around Us* is as famousₐ*as* or perhaps

even more famous than her *Silent Spring*.   ___*as*___

1. Some ecology-minded readers appreciate Rachel Carson better than any writer because of her fine style. _____

2. She is remembered not only for her warnings about the dangers of insecticide poisoning but for her charming studies of the sea. _____

3. Her death from cancer in 1964, perhaps as a result of her experiments with insecticides, was both a tragedy and irony. _____

4. Another ecological writer whose fame is well established and whose words widely read is Barry Commoner. _____

5. Barry Commoner is especially interested and skillful at describing the dangers of fallout from nuclear testing. _____

6. People have and probably will say for many years to come that Commoner's *Science and Survival* should be required reading for anyone concerned about ecology. _____

7. In the chapter "Sorcerer's Apprentice" Commoner shows the hazards associated with many scientific advances have been overlooked. _____

8. Fallout from nuclear testing, he claims, will be as much a threat in the future as the past because radioactive pollutants will be around for generations. _____

9. The world people live in the future is determined by what we do to it today. _____

10. Commoner advises that we look closely and evaluate the risks associated with technological advances before we commit ourselves to action. _____

11. At one time the dangers associated with a particular technological development—like the steamboat, for example—were relegated to a few people, not entire population. _____

12. If a boiler exploded on a steamboat, one person, or even several people, might be killed, but the danger would not be widespread enough to affect an area as large or even larger than an entire country. _____

13. Clearly a malfunction of a nuclear reactor is more serious than a steam engine. _____

14. An explosion involving nuclear power may affect people in other countries as well as the United States. _____

15. Barry Commoner does not call for a halt to scientific progress but rather evaluation of the risks involved in a scientific development before action is taken. _____

16. According to Commoner, our mistake in the past was we undertook projects without thinking about their possible ill effects. _____

Unity and Logical Thinking   u 23

23

Bring into the sentence only related ideas and pertinent details. Complete each thought logically.

23a   Unrelated ideas should be developed in separate sentences.

If ideas are related, they should be expressed in such a way that the relationship is immediately clear to the reader.

UNRELATED   Mr. Jones serves on the school board, and he is an engineer.
IMPROVED   Mr. Jones serves on the school board. He is an engineer.   OR
            Mr. Jones, an engineer, serves on the school board.   [Unity
            secured by subordination of one idea]

23b   Excessive detail should not be allowed to obscure the central thought of the sentence.

Such detail, if important, should be developed in separate sentences; otherwise it should be omitted.

OVERLOADED   When I was just a child, living in my parents' house, which
             burned down long ago, I had already read most of the novels in
             the public library, which was close by.
BETTER   When I was just a child, I had already read most of the novels
             in the nearby public library.   [If the writer considers other
             details important, he may add them in a second sentence: "I was
             then living in my parents' home, which burned down long ago."]

23c   Mixed, obscure, or illogical constructions should be avoided.

MIXED   This uprising must be reined in or it will boil over.   [Figure of a
         spirited horse being controlled plus figure of liquid becoming over-
         heated]
BETTER   This uprising must be reined in or it will get out of control.   [Figure
         of a spirited horse carried throughout]
MIXED   Because he was ambitious caused him to leave the town.   [An adverb
         clause, a part of a complex sentence, is here used as the subject of a
         simple sentence.]
CLEAR   His ambition caused him to leave the town.   [Single sentence]   OR
         Because he was ambitious he left the town.   [Adverb clause retained;
         main clause added to complete the complex sentence]

143

MIXED	A hypocrite is when a person is insincere. [Avoid the *is when* or *is where* construction. A *when* clause, used as an adverb, cannot be substituted for a noun.]
LOGICAL	A hypocrite is an insincere person.
MIXED	To ostracize is where a person is excluded from a group. [Adverb clause misused as a noun]
LOGICAL	To ostracize a person is to exclude him from a group.
ILLOGICAL	She wouldn't hardly say a word. [Double negative]
LOGICAL	She would hardly say a word.

Subordination **sub 24**

24

Use subordination to relate ideas concisely and effectively; use coordination only to give ideas equal emphasis.

24a In general a related series of short, choppy sentences should be combined into longer units in which the lesser ideas are properly subordinated.

| CHOPPY | The Australian kangaroo is a marsupial. He can move at thirty miles an hour and clear most fences with ease. |
| BETTER | The Australian kangaroo, a marsupial, can move at thirty miles an hour and clear most fences with ease. |

24b Two or more main clauses should not be carelessly joined by *and*, *so*, or other coordinating words when one clause should be subordinated to another.

Coordination should be used only for ideas of equal importance.

INEFFECTIVE	My car brakes failed and (OR so) I had a wreck. [Two main clauses]
BETTER	Because my car brakes failed, I had a wreck.
ACCEPTABLE	The movie was good, but I did not enjoy it. [Coordination used to stress equally the movie and the reaction]
USUALLY BETTER	Although the movie was good, I did not enjoy it. [Stress on one of the two ideas—the reaction]

24c Avoid illogical as well as awkward subordination.

| ABSURD | When the ball hit me, I leaned out the window. |
| LOGICAL | When I leaned out the window, the ball hit me. OR The ball hit me when I leaned out the window. |

NAME _____ SCORE _____

DIRECTIONS   In the blank at the right of each of the following sentences enter *1, 2,* or *3* to indicate whether the chief difficulty is (1) joining of unrelated ideas, (2) use of excessive detail, or (3) mixed, obscure, or illogical construction. Then rewrite the sentences to make them effective.

EXAMPLE

Through
~~The~~ reading ~~of~~ ecological studies ~~is where~~ one gets the facts he
needs to make wise decisions about the environment.   *3*

1. There are many good ecological studies, and Robert and Leona Train Rienow have written a book called *Moment in the Sun.*   _____

2. Because Americans seemingly have all the material blessings possible is why the Rienows call this period our moment in the sun.   _____

3. Although the sun may be at its zenith now, with Americans enjoying the most affluent society in man's history, the period of the zenith of opulence is only a momentary blessing that will quickly begin to recede, even as the sun sets, unless Americans, who too often take things for granted, guard their environment more carefully.   _____

4. According to the Rienows, Americans cannot shut their eyes to the warnings heard throughout the land.   _____

5. Two of the warnings to American society are when our population continues to expand and when this expanding population continues to demand an ever increasing standard of living.   _____

6. In Japan was the scene of an interesting computerized study of the use of services.   _____

7. The Japanese studied the number of people a passenger train can accommodate in summer and in winter, and in winter

people wear overcoats so the train can accommodate 20 percent fewer passengers. _____

8. The effects of overcoats on services is but one of the issues sociologists must turn their mind to if the population continues to increase. _____

9. Wearing thermal underwear may be the solution to this population problem, but there are other sociological fires smoldering that are not so easily destroyed. _____

10. Industry may be happy with our increasing population, and the more people there are, the more goods there are that are needed. _____

11. At some point, however, the goods demanded by our increasing population, which is expected to number about 350 million by the year 2000, will be too much for our country, already overcrowded with highways and buildings that are continuously being added to at an alarming rate, to supply. _____

12. By the year 2000 is when construction will have increased five times and automobile production more than twice over what it is today. _____

13. The land will indeed be too crowded with buildings and with cars to provide the life style people now enjoy, and where can 244 million cars be parked? _____

14. The increasing world population is another shadow the Rienows see as a threat to our peak of prosperity. _____

15. Since there will be more and more hungry people in the world is a problem we must face. _____

16. By the year 2000 the various underdeveloped continents will have increased their population to almost unbelievable numbers, and Asia will have as many people as the entire world now has. _____

NAME _____ SCORE _____

DIRECTIONS   Combine each of the following groups of short sentences into one effective sentence. Express the most important idea in the main clause and put lesser ideas in subordinate clauses, phrases, or words. Use coordination only for ideas of equal importance.

EXAMPLE

The *Today* show observed Earth Week, 1970. The show was moderated by Hugh Downs. It featured famous ecologists. Margaret Mead, Paul Ehrlich, and Barry Commoner were some of the ecologists featured on the *Today* show.

Observing Earth Week, 1970, the Today show, moderated by Hugh Downs, featured such famous ecologists as Margaret Mead, Paul Ehrlich, and Barry Commoner.

1. The theme of the show was "New World or No World." It expressed a point of view. This point of view was that man will have to turn his life upside-down to continue his existence.

_____

_____

_____

_____

2. Hugh Downs traced the history of our attitude toward the environment. This attitude is that man is the master of the earth and all things on it. He traced the attitude back to the days of Moses.

_____

_____

_____

_____

3. The Greeks had a profound respect for nature. They evidenced this respect in the temples they dedicated to the gods. The gods, they believed, were a part of nature.

_____

_____

_____

_____

4. Greek religion recognized a close tie between man and nature. The Judaeo-Christian religion separated man and nature. It made man the master of the earth and all things on it.

_____

_____

_____

_____

5. Several men preached about the sacredness of nature. Two of these men were St. Francis of Assisi and Jean Jacques Rousseau. Their words went unheeded. Man plunged headlong into the task of subduing the earth and all other living things.

_____

_____

_____

_____

NAME _____ SCORE _____

DIRECTIONS   Combine each of the following groups of short sentences into one effective sentence. Express the most important idea in the main clause and put lesser ideas in subordinate clauses, phrases, or words. Use coordination only for ideas of equal importance.

1. One of the guests on the *Today* show's presentation of "New World or No World" was Dr. Paul Ehrlich. Dr. Ehrlich is a biologist at Stanford University. He wrote a book called *The Population Bomb*. The book is a provocative one.

_____

_____

_____

_____

2. Dr. Ehrlich claims to believe that something can be done to save mankind. He is doubtful that much will be done. He is pessimistic because the programs that must be carried out are rather drastic. They will involve a change in the life style of the average American.

_____

_____

_____

_____

3. Dr. Ehrlich believes that the population explosion is as serious in the United States as anywhere else. He recommends that the President tell the people they should have no more than two children. They should preferably have one or none. They should limit their families in this way if they want to be patriotic and responsible citizens.

_____

_____

4. Another step Dr. Ehrlich recommends involves legislation concerning the automobile. This legislation would restrict the size of automobiles. Small cars would reduce our traffic and smog problems.

5. The government may not enact necessary environmental legislation. In that case Dr. Ehrlich recommends that the people act. He urges the people to defeat candidates who will not take a firm stand on ecology. And they should support those candidates who will enact necessary legislation.

NAME _____ SCORE _____

DIRECTIONS   Rewrite each of the following stringy sentences to make one effective sentence. Express the most important idea in the main clause and put lesser ideas in subordinate clauses, phrases, or words. Use coordination only for ideas of equal importance.

EXAMPLE

Today's reporter at large, Paul Cunningham, gave a special environmental report, and he talked about the problem of pollution in the Houston Ship Channel.

In a special environmental report, Today's reporter at large, Paul Cunningham, talked about the problem of pollution in the Houston Ship Channel.

1. Houston is an inland city, and it dredged a ship channel fifty miles long in 1914, and the city is now the third largest port in tonnage handled in the United States.

_____

_____

_____

_____

2. Waste was poured into the Houston Ship Channel, and the waste was ten times more than the channel could assimilate, so the channel became one of the most polluted bodies of water in the world.

_____

_____

_____

_____

3. A water-quality research team has tested the water in the channel, and their findings are almost unbelievable, and the findings are that sludge from the waste poured into the channel builds up at a rate of one to three feet a year.

_____

_____

_____

_____

4. Much of the pollution of the channel is industrial waste, but just as much is sewage, and both Houston and Galveston dump sewage into the channel, and these two cities are at either end of the channel.

_____

_____

_____

_____

5. The waste products in the channel destroy the marine life in the channel itself, and they also destroy the marine life in the bay, and the waste products even affect the marine life in the Gulf of Mexico.

_____

_____

_____

_____

Coherence: Misplaced Parts, Dangling Modifiers

25

Avoid needless separation of related parts of the sentence. Avoid dangling modifiers.

Every sentence should be so constructed that the relationships among its several parts will be clear to the reader at a glance. Modifiers should be placed as close as possible to the words they modify.

25a   Avoid needless separation of related parts of the sentence.

(1) In standard written English, adverbs such as *almost, only, just, even, hardly, nearly,* or *merely* are regularly placed immediately before the words they modify.

In spoken English, which tends to place these adverbs before the verb, ambiguity can be prevented by stressing the word to be modified. In written English, however, clarity is ensured only by correct placement of adverbs.

> INFORMAL   The folk singer *only* sang one song.
> GENERAL   The folk singer sang *only one song.*

(2) The position of a modifying prepositional phrase should clearly indicate what the phrase modifies.

A prepositional phrase used as an adjective nearly always immediately follows the word modified.

> MISPLACED   I gave my dress to Mary *with the low neckline.*
> CLEAR   I gave my *dress with the low neckline* to Mary.

(3) Adjective clauses should be placed near the words they modify.

> AWKWARD   He bought the vest at a men's clothing store *which cost only five dollars.*   [*Which* does not refer to *store.*]
> CLEAR   At a men's clothing store, he bought the *vest, which cost only five dollars.*   [*Which* refers to *vest.*]

(4) Avoid "squinting" constructions—modifiers that may refer either to a preceding or to a following word.

> SQUINTING   I decided *on the next day* to take a vacation.
> CLEAR   I decided *to take a vacation on the next day.*   OR   *On the next day I decided* to take a vacation.

(5) Avoid awkward separation of parts of verb phrases and awkward splitting of infinitives.

AWKWARD	There sat my grandmother, whom we *had* early that morning *put* on the plane.
IMPROVED	There sat my grandmother, whom we *had put* on the plane early that morning.
AWKWARD	She had decided *to,* in a moment of fear, *get off* the plane.
IMPROVED	In a moment of fear she had decided *to get off* the plane. [In general avoid the "split" infinitive unless it is needed for smoothness or clarity.]

Note: Although all split infinitives were once considered questionable, those which are not awkward are now acceptable.

25b   Avoid dangling modifiers.

A participle, a gerund, an infinitive, or an elliptical clause or phrase should have in the same sentence a word to which it is clearly and logically related. Otherwise, it is said to "dangle." Eliminate such errors (1) by recasting the sentence to make the dangling element agree with the subject of the main clause or (2) by expanding the phrase or elliptical clause into a subordinate clause. (Do not mistake a transitional expression like *to sum up* for a dangling modifier: see **12b**.)

(1)   Dangling participial phrase

DANGLING	*Shouldering our knapsacks,* the hike began. [*Shouldering* does not refer to *knapsacks,* nor to any other word in the sentence.]
IMPROVED	*Shouldering* (OR *Having shouldered*) *our knapsacks, we* began the hike. [*Shouldering* refers to *we,* the subject of the sentence.]
EXPANDED	*After we had shouldered our knapsacks,* the hike began. [Participial phrase expanded into a clause]

(2)   Dangling gerund phrase

DANGLING	*On arriving at the river,* the current was frightening.
IMPROVED	*On arriving at the river, we* were frightened by the current.
EXPANDED	*When we arrived at the river,* the current was frightening.

(3)   Dangling infinitive phrase

DANGLING	*To hike well,* endurance is needed.
IMPROVED	*To hike well, one* needs endurance.
EXPANDED	*If one is to hike well,* endurance is needed.

(4)   Dangling elliptical clause (or phrase)

An elliptical clause—that is, a clause with an implied subject and verb—"dangles" unless the implied subject is the same as that of the main clause.

DANGLING	*When only a baby* (OR *At the age of six months*), her father taught her to swim. [*She was* is implied in the elliptical clause.]
IMPROVED	*When only a baby* (OR *At the age of six months*), *she* was taught to swim by her father.
EXPANDED	*When she was only a baby* (OR *When she was six months old*), her father taught her to swim.

Misplaced parts

NAME _____ SCORE _____

DIRECTIONS   Some of the sentences below are incoherent because of misplaced parts. First, circle the misplaced word, phrase, or clause; then draw an arrow indicating the correct placement. In the blank at the right, enter (1) the word or (2) the first and last words of the phrase or clause. (Change capitalization and add punctuation if necessary.) If the sentence is correct, write *C* in the blank at the right.

EXAMPLE

Hugh Downs talked with Ralph Nader about air pollution, on one *Today* show.   *on–show*

1. Ralph Nader has throughout our country become a well-known name. _____

2. He is prone to whenever he senses a danger to the public speak out on consumer products. _____

3. The automobile has been under attack by Nader for several years which he feels is a danger to the public. _____

4. Nader thinks the automobile is both unsafe to the occupants of the car and to the general public. _____

5. Partly through his efforts safety devices were installed in cars such as seat belts. _____

6. Nader's concern has been the automobile as a major air polluter lately. _____

7. Nader claims that automobiles "consistently and flagrantly violate the Federal Air Pollution Standards" now coming off the assembly lines. _____

8. Nader advises the public to not be fooled by the automobile industry's public relations advertising. _____

9. According to Nader, the technology is available for the production of automobiles that are both efficient and pollution-free now. _____

10. Nader claims that facts are being suppressed about the technology available for improving automobiles by the industry and by the government. _____

11. The public only knows what it is told by the automobile industry. _____

12. Nader says that today's gasolines produce five major pollutants which are labeled "clean." _____

13. Furthermore, rubber tires have not been investigated at all by the industry's researchers which are possibly among the worst polluters. _____

14. In Nader's view, the automobile industry has on false or misleading advertising spent millions of dollars. _____

15. But the industry has just spent a fraction of this amount on research to improve the automobile. _____

16. The current automobile, which the American public buys so willingly, is only an antique model in comparison with what it could be. _____

NAME _____ SCORE _____

DIRECTIONS   A dangling modifier fails to refer clearly and logically to some word in the sentence. In the following sentences correct any dangling modifier by (1) recasting or rearranging the sentence to make the dangling element agree with the subject of the main clause or by (2) expanding the phrase or elliptical clause into a subordinate clause. Be sure, in the course of correcting the sentences, that you use *both* methods of correction. Show how you have made the correction by writing *subject* or *sub. clause* in the blank at the right. If the sentence is correct, write *C* in the blank at the right.

EXAMPLES

the Today show interviewed

Continuing its Earth Week observance,ˌDr. Margaret Mead

and Dr. René Dubos,~~were interviewed on the *Today* show.~~   *subject*

they were

When,ˌquestioned about what man should do to improve his

environment, their primary concern was a change in pub-

lic attitude.   *sub. clause*

1. To be sure, public involvement is the all-important first step toward improving our environment, Dr. Dubos and Dr. Mead pointed out.   _____

2. Knowing what to do, perhaps appropriate action will be taken.   _____

3. Using common sense, one pattern of behavior that helps to destroy our environment is immediately apparent.   _____

4. Too concerned about convenience, overpackaging is one thing we practice.   _____

5. We put packages inside packages, congratulating ourselves on the neat appearance of the product.   _____

6. Especially fond of see-through packages, plastic wrappings are extensively used.   _____

7. A real pollution problem is caused by this kind of packaging, not decomposing as paper products would.   _____

8. As Dr. Dubos put it, we must "eliminate all the junk with which we load our lives," overpackaging serving as one example of what he called junk. _____

9. Agreeing with Dr. Dubos, a similar call to action was sounded by Dr. Margaret Mead. _____

10. When confronted with the facts about the state of our environment, extreme pessimism and hopelessness may result. _____

11. To make progress, this kind of attitude must be overcome. _____

12. Frustration is a natural response to our environmental situation, the problem of pollution seemingly having developed overnight. _____

13. Although a serious problem, we can nevertheless cope with pollution. _____

14. Equally dangerous, we must avoid a Pollyanna attitude. _____

15. We may be tempted to settle back and forget the environment, satisfied that we have watched a series of programs on ecology. _____

16. To conclude, we have to develop a real appreciation for our home; we must, as Margaret Mead said, "learn to cherish this earth and cherish it as something that is fragile." _____

26

Parallel ideas should be expressed in parallel structure.

26a Coordinate ideas are clearer to the reader when they are expressed in parallel structure.

To express coordinate ideas a noun should be balanced with a noun, an active verb with an active verb, an infinitive with an infinitive, a subordinate clause with a subordinate clause, a main clause with a main clause.

> AWKWARD Let us remember *his love* and *that he was kind.*   [Noun paralleled with a subordinate clause]
>
> PARALLEL *Let us remember* ‖ *his love* and
>   ‖ *his kindness.*
>
> OR
>
> Let us remember ‖ *that he loved us* and
>   ‖ *that he was kind.*

> AWKWARD *To sleep* and *eating* were his main occupations.   [Infinitive paralleled with a gerund]
>
> PARALLEL ‖ *To sleep* and
>   ‖ *to eat*
> were his main occupations.
>
> OR
>
>   ‖ *Eating* and
>   ‖ *sleeping*
> were his main occupations.

26b Repetition of a preposition, an article, an auxiliary verb, the sign of the infinitive, or the introductory word of a long phrase or clause is often necessary to make the parallel clear.

> AWKWARD I envy the mayor *for his privileges,* but not *his responsibilities.*
>
> IMPROVED I envy the mayor ‖ *for his privileges,* but not
>   ‖ *for his responsibilities.*

> AWKWARD At the party I talked to *a doctor* and *lawyer.*
>
> IMPROVED At the party I talked to ‖ *a doctor* and
>   ‖ *a lawyer.*

26c Correlatives (*either . . . or, neither . . . nor, both . . . and, not only . . . but also, whether . . . or*) should be followed by elements that are parallel in form.

> FAULTY She was *not only pretty but also knew how to dress well.*   [Adjective paralleled with a verb]
>
> BETTER She was ‖ *not only pretty*
>
> BETTER   ‖ *but also well dressed.*

27

Avoid needless shifts in point of view.

27a   Needless shift in tense

SHIFT   The boy *ate* the candy and *throws* the wrapper on the floor. [Shift from past tense to present tense]

BETTER   The boy *ate* the candy and *threw* the wrapper on the floor. [Both verbs in the past tense]

27b   Needless shift in mood

SHIFT   First *listen* intently and then you *should take* notes. [Shift from imperative to indicative mood]

BETTER   First *listen* intently and then *take* notes. [Both verbs in the imperative mood]

27c   Needless shift in subject or voice

A shift in subject often involves a shift in voice. A shift in voice nearly always involves a shift in subject.

SHIFT   Ann liked tennis, but ping-pong was also enjoyed by her. [The subject shifts from *Ann* to *ping-pong*. The voice shifts from active to passive.]

BETTER   Ann liked tennis, but she also enjoyed ping-pong. [One subject only. Both verbs are active.]

27d   Needless shift in person

SHIFT   If *a person* reads well, *you* will probably succeed in school. [Shift from third person to second person]

BETTER   If *a person* reads well, *he* will probably succeed in school.

27e   Needless shift in number

SHIFT   *One* should vote to express *their* political views. [Shift from singular *one* to plural *their*]

BETTER   *One* should vote to express *his* (OR *one's*) political views.

27f   Needless shift from indirect to direct discourse

SHIFT   Sue asked *whether I knew* the nominee and *will he be* a good sheriff. [Mixed indirect and direct discourse]

BETTER   Sue asked *whether I knew* the nominee and *whether he would be* a good sheriff. [Indirect discourse]   OR
Sue asked, *"Do you know* the nominee? *Will he be* a good sheriff?" [Direct discourse]

NAME _____ SCORE _____

DIRECTIONS In each of the following sentences underscore the parts having parallel ideas that should be expressed in parallel structure. Revise each sentence to make the parts parallel, and enter the key word or words of the revision in the blank at the right.

EXAMPLE

On Earth Day, 1970, many cities staged demon-
strations that were both <u>dramatic</u> and ~~some-~~ *extraordinary.*

~~thing out of the ordinary.~~   *extraordinary*

1. In New York, for example, people gathered at Union Square to breathe fresh air from a huge bubble and for a survival kit. _____

2. Something even more surprising and which attracted many sightseers was the scrubbing of Union Square. _____

3. Part of Fourteenth Street was closed to motor vehicles and allowing people only on foot or in nonmotorized conveyances. _____

4. In the closed area people could travel in electric cars, or bicycles, or even roller skates. _____

5. Part of Fifth Avenue, too, was closed to automobiles to show concern for the environment and as a protest against automobile pollutants. _____

6. In Philadelphia demonstrators signed not a Declaration of Independence but rather they put their names on a Declaration of Interdependence to indicate their recognition of the vital link between man and nature. _____

7. Smaller towns as well as cities that are large metropolises celebrated Earth Day.

   _____

8. In Jamestown, New York, the Kiwanis Club demonstrated pollution in a strange way and which was quite ingenious.

   _____

9. Twenty tons of sand were dumped in a downtown area to show adults as well as the children how much dirt falls in a square mile of the city during a thirty-day period of maximum pollution.

   _____

10. In Ashtabula, Ohio, demonstrators conducted a funeral service for unborn babies who will begin life in a polluted environment and possibly victimized by the pollution.

    _____

11. In the NASA area, near Houston, large groups of mothers with their children could be seen collecting litter along the highways, in the shopping areas, and the banks of Clear Lake.

    _____

12. Some political leaders warned that people should not focus entirely on pollution but to broaden their concern to include other areas of national neglect.

    _____

13. One often does not know whether he should focus on one problem or to direct his energy to all the problems facing the country.

    _____

14. Certainly, though, Earth Day celebrations did alert people to the state of our environment and what some of the improvements we can make are.

    _____

15. Earth Day caused many people to stop, to look around, and finally think about ecology.

    _____

Shifts in point of view

NAME _____ SCORE _____

DIRECTIONS   Indicate the kind of shift in each of the following sentences by marking in the blank at the right *a* (tense), *b* (mood), *c* (subject-voice), *d* (person), *e* (number), or *f* (discourse). Make the necessary corrections.

EXAMPLE

In the past a person was sometimes laughed at for ~~their~~ *his* efforts to

improve the environment.   *e*

1. Today when one reads about the activities of a woman like Mrs. Trudy Bernhardt, you do not laugh.   _____

2. Because Mrs. Bernhardt was concerned about the deer population in the Everglades, she dons high boots and goes into the swamps to help rescue fawns threatened by flood waters.   _____

3. High water drowns many fawns and much of the food supply is also eliminated by the water.   _____

4. During the floods of 1970, when the foliage was stripped away up to the tree line, the fawns, unable to reach the food supply, die of starvation.   _____

5. When one reads that during the last seven years the deer population in the Everglades has diminished from thirty-five hundred to fewer than four hundred, they realize how important the efforts of people like Mrs. Bernhardt are.   _____

6. When we hear the story of Mrs. Bernhardt and others like her who quietly work to save our wildlife, a person cannot help feeling optimistic about the future.   _____

7. In California hundreds of people worked long hours to try to save birds that have been coated with sludge from oil slicks.   _____

8. Since the birds could not fly, the people washed them until most of the sludge is removed.   _____

163

9. All over the country there are people who do not have to ask whether there is anything they can do to save their wildlife and is it worth their effort. _____

10. Wherever one lives they can discover wildlife that is threatened with extinction. _____

11. In Texas a young girl became concerned about the vanishing pelican population, and many hours of each week were spent by her working to reestablish the giant birds on Pelican Island. _____

12. In some coastal areas the inhabitants noticed the disappearance of sea turtles; consequently, they begin to work with government officials to prevent the stealing of the turtles' eggs. _____

13. An individual can always find something to do for the environment if you will look around. _____

14. We can be glad that the person who does care about wildlife is no longer labeled overly sentimental because of their concern. _____

15. Rather be thankful for these people and we should hope that others will join them. _____

16. The Declaration of Interdependence recognizes that every man is dependent not only on their fellow man but also upon every living thing in the environment. _____

Parallelism and shifts in point of view

NAME _____ SCORE _____

DIRECTIONS   In the blank after each sentence below, write *1* or *2* to indicate whether the chief defect in the sentence is (1) lack of parallelism or (2) needless shift in point of view. Make the necessary corrections.

EXAMPLES

Even as many a concerned individual is devoting ~~themselves~~ *himself* to saving the environment, so many a city, too, is making significant progress in the fight against pollution.   **2**

Through the legislation they pass, many cities are indicating ~~that~~ ~~they are aware~~ *their awareness* of pollution problems and ~~showing~~ *their* determination to eliminate them.   **1**

1. The Houston Ship Channel has been labeled filthy, contaminated, and with signs of being unsafe by pollution experts. _____

2. For several years Houston, like many other cities, ignored the pollution of its waterways and thus allowing the contamination to get out of hand. _____

3. In 1968 Houston voted against bond issues that would construct modern sewage treatment plants to eliminate nearly raw sewage from entering their ship channel, but in 1970 the city voted for the bonds. _____

4. Houston had to decide whether to spend money for the costly process of cleaning up its waterways or it could save money at the expense of the health of its community. _____

5. Other cities face the same choice, and more and more frequently they decided to pay the cost for cleaning up the environment. _____

6. London, England, is one such city, and they have not regretted the decision to spend the necessary funds for cleaner air. _____

7. For many years air pollution was so bad in London that a person with any respiratory trouble dare not leave home. _____

8. A sick or elderly individual ran the risk of actually losing their life to air pollution during certain times of the year. _____

9. In 1952 there was so much sulfur dioxide in the air that four thousand people die in six days' time. _____

10. For hundreds of years Londoners burned coal in their fireplaces, and it was a practice not easily given up by them. _____

11. Everyone knows how hard it is to change your habits. _____

12. The great smog of 1952 convinced Londoners that their health was more important than a tradition and to pass the necessary legislation to restrict fuels to smokeless solid types. _____

13. The government paid seven-tenths of the cost for purchasing a fireplace converter and to install it. _____

14. Since the passage of the Clean Air Act of 1956 visitors to London have been amazed at how much cleaner the air is and the city is more beautiful. _____

15. By 1970 there was 50 percent more sunshine in the city of London than there had been in 1960; and the stones of St. Paul's Cathedral, Trafalgar Square, and Buckingham Palace, once gray and ugly, are clean and beautiful. _____

16. Today Londoners are happier and have better health as a result of their passage of the necessary legislation to help clean up their city. _____

28

Make every pronoun refer unmistakably and definitely to its antecedent.

A pronoun has meaning only if the reader understands the antecedent (usually a noun or another pronoun) to which it refers. If the reader cannot determine the antecedent at first glance, the sentence should be recast.

28a   Avoid ambiguous reference.

Do not cause the reader to hesitate between two antecedents.

> AMBIGUOUS   Mary told Laura that she had used her perfume.   [Who had used whose perfume?]
>
> CLEAR   Mary said to Laura, "I have used your perfume."   OR   Mary said to Laura, "You have used my perfume."

28b   Avoid remote reference.

Do not refer to an antecedent too far removed from the pronoun. Usually a clear antecedent will come within the same sentence as the pronoun or in the sentence immediately preceding.

> REMOTE   The lake covers many acres. Near the shore, water lilies grow in profusion, spreading out their green leaves and sending up white blossoms on slender stems. *It* is well stocked with fish.   [The pronoun *it* is too far removed from its antecedent *lake*.]
>
> IMPROVED   . . . The *lake* is well stocked with fish.   [Repetition of the antecedent *lake*]
>
> VAGUE   Jon went to the beach to look for a starfish to add to his collection. *It* was usually covered with shells.   [Temporarily confusing: the antecedent of *it* is not clear until the reader finishes the sentence.]
>
> CLEAR   Jon went to the *beach, which* was usually covered with shells, to look for a starfish to add to his collection.   [The pronoun *which* is placed next to its antecedent, *beach*.]
>
> OBSCURE   When Bob's health studio was begun, *he* asked me to be a customer.   [Reference to antecedent in the possessive case]
>
> IMPROVED   When *Bob* began his health studio, *he* asked me to be a customer.

28c   Use broad reference only with discretion.

As a rule avoid *broad* reference (1) to the general idea of a preceding clause or sentence, (2) to a noun not expressed but merely inferred from a verb or some other word, or (3) to some indefinite antecedent by the use of *they, you,* or *it.*[1] That is, ordinarily use a pronoun only when it has as its antecedent some specific noun or word used as a noun.

VAGUE   Many college students travel to Europe for the summer. This gives them the opportunity to learn a second language and to experience a different culture from the one they have grown up in. [*This* has no antecedent.]

CLEAR   The many college students who travel to Europe for the summer have an opportunity to learn a second language and to experience a different culture from the one they have grown up in. [The vague pronoun is eliminated.]

VAGUE   In one of Wordsworth's poems it tells about a young man who is corrupted by city life.

CLEAR   One of Wordsworth's poems tells about a young man who is corrupted by city life.

COLLOQUIAL   At college they expect students to take care of themselves.

CLEAR   At college students are expected to take care of themselves.

28d   Avoid the confusion arising from the repetition in the same sentence of a pronoun referring to different antecedents.

CONFUSING   Although it is very hot by the lake, it looks inviting. [The first *it* is an indefinite pronoun; the second *it* refers to *lake.*]

CLEAR   Although it is very hot by the lake, the water looks inviting.

CONFUSING   We should have prepared for our examinations earlier. It is too late to do it now.

CLEAR   We should have prepared for our examinations earlier. It is too late to prepare now.

---

[1] Informal English allows much latitude in the use of antecedents that must be inferred from the context. Even standard or formal English sometimes accepts the general idea of a clause as an antecedent when the reference is unmistakable. But it is generally wise for the inexperienced writer to make each of his pronouns refer to a specific noun or pronoun.

NAME _____ SCORE _____

DIRECTIONS   In the following sentences mark a capital *V* through each pronoun that makes a vague reference and enter the pronoun in the blank at the right. Recast the sentence or sentences to clarify the meaning.

EXAMPLE   *like those in the communes,*

Some people ⌃try to establish a new relationship with nature by leaving civilization. ~~The communes are an example of~~ ~~this~~.   *this*

1. Even during the nineteenth century there were people who did not appreciate the signs of progress that were most noticeable in the urban areas and who sought to escape it.   _____

2. Henry David Thoreau wanted to escape the smokestacks and the busyness of modern civilization, which is why he went to Walden Pond.   _____

3. Seeking "to confront only the essentials of life," Thoreau knew that if he did not do it while he was young, he would never have the opportunity again.   _____

4. Ralph Waldo Emerson talked with Thoreau about living apart from civilization, but he did not follow his example.   _____

5. In *Walden* it tells about Thoreau's experiences with nature.   _____

6. They say that Thoreau did not spend all his time apart from friends and civilization.   _____

7. This may be true, but Thoreau did spend most of his two years at Walden in contact with only the land and the wildlife.   _____

8. He built his own house and grew most of his food, which gave him a real sense of independence.   _____

9. Today there are people who follow Thoreau's advice. This is because they seek something which, to them, the city has destroyed. _____

10. Unlike the people who try to improve the city, those who follow Thoreau's example find it futile to work for reform and so decide to escape it. _____

11. Some seek privacy in other less civilized countries while others go to isolated parts of our own country for this. _____

12. Many communes are hidden away from civilization. Mountains and forests serve as protectors of privacy and independence. They often are inaccessible by car. _____

13. The Hog Farmers' Commune can be reached only on foot, which discourages sightseers and other interlopers. _____

14. Still more independent individuals tell those who live in communes that they seek more isolation than their way of life provides. _____

15. They find contentment only in total separation from mankind that they seek. _____

16. One of these rare individuals in Tennessee has lived for many years in a cave which he has entirely decorated with furnishings made by his own hands. He claims this provides all the shelter and comforts he needs. _____

29

Select words and arrange the parts of the sentence to give emphasis to important ideas.

29a   Gain emphasis by placing important words at the beginning or end of the sentence—especially at the end.

WEAK   The Senate will now pass the bill, in all probability. [The weakest part of the sentence is given the most emphatic position—the end.]

EMPHATIC   In all probability, the Senate will now pass the bill. [Strong end] OR The Senate, in all probability, will now pass the bill. [Most emphatic—strong beginning and end]

29b   Gain emphasis by changing loose sentences into periodic sentences.

A sentence that holds the reader in suspense until the end is called *periodic;* one that makes a complete statement and then adds details is called *loose.* Both types of sentences are good. The loose sentence, more commonly used, makes for easy reading. But the periodic sentence, by reserving the main idea until the end, is more emphatic. Note the difference in tone in the following sentences.

LOOSE   Remember names if you want to run for public office. [A clear sentence]

PERIODIC   If you want to run for public office, remember names. [More emphatic]

Note that this technique is an extension of the principle presented in **29a**.

29c   Gain emphasis by arranging ideas in the order of climax.

UNEMPHATIC   He pledged her his love, his time, and his money.
EMPHATIC   He pledged her his money, his time, and his love.

29d   Gain emphasis by using the active instead of the passive voice.

WEAK   Daily calls to his fiancée were made by him.
STRONG   He made daily calls to his fiancée.

29e   Gain emphasis by using balanced sentences.

UNBALANCED   It is human to err, but to forgive is divine.
BALANCED   To err is human, to forgive divine.

30

Vary the length and structure of your sentences to make your whole composition pleasing and effective.

A monotonous repetition of the same sentence structure and the same sentence length throughout a paragraph will tire the reader. The effective writer changes the pace of his composition by varying the length and the structure of his sentences, and by varying the beginnings, as this short paragraph from Jacques Barzun's "In Favor of Capital Punishment" illustrates:

> But why kill? I am ready to believe the statistics tending to show that the prospect of his own death does not stop the murderer. For one thing he is often a blind egotist, who cannot conceive the possibility of his own death. For another, detection would have to be infallible to deter the more imaginative who, although afraid, think they can escape discovery. Lastly, as Shaw long ago pointed out, hanging the wrong man will deter as effectively as hanging the right one. So, once again, why kill? If I agree that moral progress means an increasing respect for human life, how can I oppose abolition?[1]

30a   Vary the sentence chiefly by opening with an adverb or an adverb phrase or clause.

> ADVERB   The quarterback listened to the coach's instructions. *Then* the team discussed the upcoming play in the huddle.
> ADVERB PHRASE   *After listening to the coach's instructions,* the quarterback discussed the upcoming play in the huddle.
> ADVERB CLAUSE   *After the quarterback had listened to the coach's instructions,* he discussed the upcoming play in the huddle.

30b   Vary the sentence by opening with a prepositional or a participial phrase.

> PREPOSITIONAL PHRASE   *In the huddle* the team discussed the upcoming play.
> PARTICIPIAL PHRASE   *Huddling at mid-field,* the team discussed the upcoming play.

30c   Vary the sentence by opening with a coordinating conjunction such as *and, but, or, nor,* or *yet* when the conjunction can be used to show the proper relation of the sentence to the preceding sentence.

> When the quarterback returned to the huddle with the coach's instructions, the team discussed the upcoming play with enthusiasm. *And* they came up to the line ready to make the double reverse gain them a touchdown.

---

[1] "In Favor of Capital Punishment," *American Scholar,* 31, 2 (Spring 1962), 183.

NAME _____ SCORE _____

DIRECTIONS   Enter *a, b, c, d,* or *e* in the blank at the right to indicate that each of the following sentences is unemphatic chiefly because of (a) ineffective placement of important words, (b) the use of loose instead of periodic structure, (c) the lack of climactic order, (d) the use of the passive instead of the active voice, or (e) the lack of proper balance. Revise the sentences to make them emphatic.

EXAMPLE

To be sure,
  ʌ "Ñot everyone is ready to give up on the cities and industrial-

ization/. to be sure.   *a*

1. There will be nowhere to run if the present rate of pollution continues.   _____

2. The efforts of some people are expended toward improving the environment around them.   _____

3. The majority of people register no protest of any kind, however.   _____

4. They show no regard for the present environmental crisis by their speech, their actions, or their thoughts.   _____

5. With an apathetic public, pollution will continue; environmental progress will be made with a concerned public.   _____

6. Political leaders at all levels of government—national, state, and local—respond to the issues that they feel the public is concerned about.   _____

7. Our political representatives pass environmental legislation when the public demands it.   _____

8. Ecology is fast becoming a major plank in the political platform, undoubtedly.   _____

9. To speak in favor of ecology is a safe political course; it is less safe to take action.   _____

10. Politicians are naturally reluctant to call upon the public to make sacrifices for the environment because they want to be reelected.   _____

DIRECTIONS The following are memorable quotations from some of our most out-spoken environmentalists. Enter *1, 2,* or *3* in the blanks at the right to classify the sentences rhetorically as (1) loose (2) periodic, or (3) balanced. (See **29b** and **29e**.)

1. Unfortunately, if the fad is only a fad, and if we fail to turn the fad into direct action, we die. —STEPHANIE MILLS   _____

2. Today the use a man makes of his land cannot be left to his private decision alone, since eventually it is bound to affect everybody else. —JOHN FISCHER   _____

3. We are producing people faster than we can feed them, just as the English economic philosopher Thomas Malthus pre-dicted in 1798 that we would. —GEORGE MC GOVERN   _____

4. Yet unless trends now gathering force are checked, the Mal-thusian nightmare will become a reality. —GEORGE MC GOVERN   _____

5. Land is wealth; land is power; land is life itself. But land is finite. —WILLIAM E. TOWELL   _____

6. If the smog had appeared in Los Angeles overnight, people would have fled gibbering into the hills. —PAUL R. EHRLICH   _____

7. The more we feed, the more they breed. —ROBERT and LEONA TRAIN RIENOW   _____

8. While one group of scientists studies ways to provide the air for the first human visitors to the moon, another tries to learn why we are fouling the air that the rest of us must breathe on earth. —BARRY COMMONER   _____

9. Thus is born the stream of rejects which become the nation's solid wastes—overwhelming mountains of the debris of afflu-ence which threaten the cleanliness, safety and beauty of our land resources and become what is now known as "the third pollution." —ARTHUR HANDLEY   _____

10. All Americans, not only the ardent, hard-working conserva-tionists, will have to participate responsibly in caring for the land. —MARGARET MEAD   _____

NAME _____ SCORE _____

DIRECTIONS   Write sentences to illustrate the various types specified below.

1. a simple sentence (**1e**)

2. a compound sentence (**1e**)

3. a simple sentence with a compound predicate (**12a**)

4. a complex sentence (**1e**)

5. a compound-complex sentence (**1e**)

6. a sentence beginning with an adverb phrase (**30a**)

7. the same sentence beginning with a prepositional phrase (**30b**)

8. the same sentence beginning with an adverb clause (**30a**)

9. the same sentence beginning with an adverb (**30a**)

10. the same sentence beginning with a participial phrase (**30b**)

11. the same sentence beginning with a coordinating conjunction (**30c**)

12. the same sentence beginning with a different coordinating conjunction (**30c**)

13. a loose sentence (**29b**)

NAME _____ SCORE _____

14. a balanced sentence (**29e**)

15. a periodic sentence (**29b**)

Individual Spelling List

Write in this list every word that you misspell—in spelling tests (see pages 121–28), in themes, or in any other written work. Add pages as needed.

NO.	WORD (CORRECTLY SPELLED)	WORD (SPELLED BY SYLLABLES) WITH TROUBLE SPOT CIRCLED	REASON FOR ERROR [1]
	considerable	con·sid'·er·a·ble	*a*
1			
2			
3			
4			
5			
6			
7			
8			
9			
10			
11			
12			
13			
14			
15			
16			
17			
18			
19			

[1] See pages 119–20 for a discussion of the chief reasons for misspelling. Indicate the reason for your misspelling by writing *a, b, c, d, e, f,* or *g* in this column.

a = Mispronunciation
b = Confusion of words similar in sound
c = Error in adding prefixes or suffixes
d = Confusion of *ei* and *ie*

e = Error in forming the plural
f = Error in using hyphens
g = Any other reason for misspelling

NO.	WORD (CORRECTLY SPELLED)	WORD (SPELLED BY SYLLABLES) WITH TROUBLE SPOT CIRCLED	REASON FOR ERROR
20			
21			
22			
23			
24			
25			
26			
27			
28			
29			
30			
31			
32			
33			
34			
35			
36			
37			
38			
39			
40			
41			
42			
43			
44			
45			